More praise for
THE GREAT HEART WAY

"I find that the Great Heart method skillfully addresses
the fundamental issue of practicing with hidden emotional
issues. The value of Great Heart is that it lays out a clear
method with vivid and compelling evidence of how
it works. I wholeheartedly endorse this book."
—Wendy Egyoku Nakao, Abbot, Zen Center of Los Angeles

"Incisive, important, and without pretense.
It is a skillful offering, adaptable by individuals
as well teachers and leaders of groups."
—Pat Enkyo O'Hara, Ph.D., Abbot, Village Zendo

"*The Great Heart Way* will help people to resolve
deep-seated issues that may not be accessible
through traditional meditation alone."
—Joan Halifax, Roshi, Ph.D., author of *The Fruitful Darkness*

"An important book. I highly recommend it for all seekers."
—Anne Seisen Saunders, Abbot, Sweetwater Zen Center

"Eminently practical and optimistic."
—Jean Smith, author of *Now! The Art of Being Truly Present*

THE GREAT HEART WAY

*How to Heal Your Life
and Find Self-Fulfillment*

ILIA SHINKO PEREZ
GERRY SHISHIN WICK

WISDOM PUBLICATIONS • BOSTON

Wisdom Publications
199 Elm Street
Somerville, MA 02144 USA
www.wisdompubs.org

Library of Congress Cataloging-in-Publication Data
Perez, Ilia Shinko.
 The great heart way : how to heal your life and find self-fulfillment
/ Ilia Shinko Perez, Gerry Shishin Wick.
     p. cm.
 Includes bibliographical references and index.
 ISBN 0-86171-513-6 (pbk. : alk. paper)
 1. Meditation. 2. Meditation—Zen Buddhism. I. Wick, Gerry
Shishin. II. Title.
 BL627.P46 2007
 294.3'444—dc22

                                2006033574

ISBN 0-86171-513-6

First Printing
10 09 08 07 06
5   4   3   2   1

Cover design by PemaStudios. Interior design by Trice Atkinson. Set in Bembo 11/15 pt.

We dedicate the merits of this book
to peace in the world.

CONTENTS

Introduction
The Great Heart Way

Healing, whether of the individual, tribe, nation, or world, has been seen as the province of an outside agency—spirits, shamans, God, government, physicians, ministers, or therapists.... Many human beings are trying to find the source of healing their ailments and discontents within themselves, though many use helpers to assist them. These helpers are not seen as gurus, saviors, or physicians, but as guides, teachers, and fellow seekers.

—JOHN PIERRAKOS[1]

In these turbulent and uncertain times, the big challenge we all face is to find a deep contentment that endures through life's ups and downs. With concerns about planetary survival, threats from terrorism, wars, environmental disasters, and with major social changes in traditional values, many of our deep fears and hopes are unaddressed. We all want to lead healthy and fulfilling lives but traditional values don't give us the nurturing and solace we need. There is a popular saying, "If we don't change the direction we are going, we will end up where we are headed." Many of us feel responsible for finding new ways for helping ourselves, our relationships, and our environment.

1

The spiritual and emotional help we need for these dilemmas cannot be given to us from an outside authority nor can it be acquired in the shopping malls or on eBay. Our materialistic culture tries to convince us, through advertisements on Internet and TV and in newspapers, that the source of our contentment lies some place outside of us. If we just have more, then we will be fine. We are also told that with the right pharmaceutical, we will have the perfect life we have been looking for. We are being sold delusion and we are paying a high price for it. However, we can find contentment in the most unlikely place—in our unconscious mind. There we can find the seeds for an unlimited expansion of consciousness and spiritual evolution.

The following story synthesizes what is happening to us, to our culture, and to our planet:

The Water of Life bubbled up from a spring and flowed freely to the people of the planet. Everyone who drank of the magic water was nurtured by it. But some selfish people wanted the water for themselves. They began to fence off the spring and claim ownership of the property around it. As the less aggressive people gradually relinquished their rights, the powerful ones began charging admission and selling the water's powers.

Eventually, the water stopped flowing there and began bubbling up somewhere else. Nevertheless those in power continued selling the water, and many people never noticed its life-giving qualities were gone. Some sincere and courageous seekers, however, found a source of *living* water elsewhere. And this is the wonder of the story: the Water of Life is always flowing somewhere, waiting to be found by anyone sincere and courageous enough to seek it out.

Water is a symbol of our deepest spiritual nourishment. In this very old allegoric story, the Water of Life can also symbolize the unconscious mind. It flows even now, in this very time. When it can't be found in the old accustomed sites, it turns up in other, sometimes surprising, places—as free and nourishing as it ever was.

In a safe, practical, and revolutionary manner, using meditation and awareness as the main vehicles, *The Great Heart Way* taps into the rich material that resides in the unconscious, and unveils the barriers to inner peace, freedom, happiness, and clarity of mind. It is time to take responsibility for our lives and hurdle the barriers. William James, one of the founders of modern psychological research, wrote "Most people live …in a very restricted circle of their potential being. They make use of a very small portion of their possible consciousness, and their soul's resources in general, much like a man who, out of his whole bodily organism, should get into a habit of using and moving only his little finger."[2] Wouldn't you like to take the veil off your eyes, use your full potential and return to the long-lost home that is within you right now?

What Is the Great Heart Way?

The Great Heart Way is a non-sectarian method for authentic spiritual and personal transformation, which unifies the mind, the body, and the emotions. The teachers of this way are spiritual guides; we are recognized teachers within the Zen tradition. We are not psychotherapists and do not provide therapy. Practicing the Great Heart Way you will learn to become the healer of your own life and thus transcend the roles of patient and therapist. Psychotherapist Eugene Gendlin writes: "Human problems are by their very nature such that we are each inherently in charge of ourselves. No authority can resolve our problems or tell us how to live."[3]

The Great Heart Way is a path of personal empowerment, an optimistic approach to self-realization that helps individuals rediscover their full potential. It can be learned by anyone who wants to take responsibility for her or his life. You only need to be willing to go beyond your comfort zone and to explore unfamiliar territory. We're so conditioned to the way we create our lives that we believe that we have no control at all. We've been conditioned to believe that the external world is more real than the internal world. But through careful introspection we can discover what many scientific studies have confirmed: what's happening within us creates what's happening outside of us. Addressing and solving our inner issues will transform our external world. The more people work on resolving their inner issues the more we will contribute to creating a healthy planet.

This method is effective for persons who currently lead normal lives and want to improve their emotional and behavioral patterns. We caution those with serious mental and physical disorders, however, to seek proper medical and psychological assistance.

ORIGINS OF THE GREAT HEART WAY

The Great Heart Way was born from our many years of exploring the depths of our own heart-minds.

When we first started to practice Zen meditation, at different Zen Centers and in different decades, we were told never to bring personal problems or emotional issues into the private interview *(dokusan)* room with the Zen Master and to only talk about our meditation practice. This instruction was also emphasized in the first American book written about Zen practice, *The Three Pillars of Zen,* published in 1965, in which the editor Philip Kapleau quotes Yasutani Roshi, "All questions should relate to problems growing directly out of your practice. This naturally excludes personal problems." [4] Imagine my (Shishin's) surprise when, once I began to hold private interviews in 1980 at the request of my teacher, Maezumi Roshi, I found that students almost exclusively wanted to discuss their emotional problems. I recall telling the senior disciple, Bernie Glassman, about my observation and he said, "That is what has grabbed hold of their mind and is all they want to talk about."

The injunction against working with personal feelings has cut off access to a powerful path for self-knowledge and transformation. Based on our own experience and the studies of others[5] on the relationship between the unconscious and the physical body, we have concluded that emotions are the language of the body and are the language of the unconscious mind. In other words, to learn how to effectively work with feelings is to learn the language of the unconscious mind. We discovered that meditation, properly guided, was a direct path to uncovering one's deeper feelings and powers hidden in the unconscious mind. During the last seven years, we have been teaching our students how to work with their feelings and how to unlock their full potentiality by accessing their unconscious mind. The Great Heart Way can be practiced both independently and in conjunction with the traditional Zen training.

Historically, there have been two ways in which people misuse meditation when dealing with feelings. They use their concentration to bypass anything unpleasant that might arise, or they use it as a place to endlessly indulge feelings (including negative ones!). People who use meditation in the first way tend to become arrogant and rigid in their beliefs and if by chance they become teachers, they can become heartless and not know how to properly address personal problems with their students. People who use it in the second way spend their time spinning their wheels and keep going over the same neurotic thoughts again and again. They usually cannot persevere in deep spiritual practice and if they are asked to see beyond their neuroses, they often will leave. Through experience we have discovered that there needs to be a balance between the personal and the traditional in Zen practice.

Traditional Zen practice as imported from the East often talks about *letting go* of emotions or holding your mind like a great iron wall against all incoming thoughts and feelings. But that is only half of the story. It is said that the path of enlightenment is a path of the heart. When your heart is closed to feelings and emotions and you totally ignore them, they will keep haunting you and appearing when you least want them. They will control your life and you will feel like a victim of circumstances. We have found that there is much important work that can be done with the feelings and emotions that arise during meditation. We call this enhancement of meditation practice the Great Heart Way, since one's heart plays a major role in transforming unconscious beliefs and emotions and opening us to true compassion and wisdom.

Meditation practice can be used to bypass the personality or to address it. Motivated by the disconnect between our ability to have "deep spiritual experiences" and our *inability* to manifest that wisdom in our daily lives and personal relationships we began using our own minds as our experimental laboratories. Over time, we developed this simple and non-sectarian guide on how to use meditation to access the unconscious mind in order to understand our personal karma, to unbind our life force, and to learn to open the heart so the light of compassionate wisdom can shine through.

In developing the Great Heart Way, we confirmed our experience and our work by drawing upon the ancient wisdom of Zen masters and other spiritual teachers and the writings of eminent psychologists and psychiatrists. The instructions that we present here are useful for people of all persuasions at all levels of experience, including beginning meditators and old-timers—even those "power meditators" who are still held captive by unhealed emotional pain.

Since the Great Heart Way has been so valuable for us and for those with whom we have worked, we want to share some of our and our students' personal experiences with our readers. In order to protect their identities, we have changed the names, ages, and professions of those students who have contributed narratives and testimonials. The discussion and practices in this book are not theoretical, but rest on a firm foundation of the personal experience of those who have practiced the Great Heart Way during the past seven years.

INFLUENCE OF THE UNCONSCIOUS MIND

As you may be aware, wealth, good fortune, and material possessions do not guarantee joy and happiness; nor does becoming expert in some field—medicine, art, computers, engineering, psychology, meditation. By most standards, for example, I (Shishin) was a successful person. I earned a Ph.D. in physics, and I have practiced traditional Zen meditation for forty years; I had also taught and published in both these disciplines. But no matter what I accomplished, I never felt I was good enough. Although it was satisfying to know that I could succeed in many things I did, it was painful to discover that I did everything out of a need to demonstrate my worth to the world. Deep within me I was carrying something that told me I wasn't adequate—and I was acting as though my life depended on proving that I was.

This internal fight disturbed my sense of inner peace. It didn't matter that I had straight A's in high school, or was class valedictorian, or a state champion in swimming. It didn't matter that I won awards playing football or was successful in college. Nor did it matter that I became a successor of Zen Master Taizan Maezumi and was empowered to be an independent teacher. The thought of not being good enough would not go away.

I carried this belief into my relationships by trying to be the perfect companion or perfect husband. But this behavior was not always appropriate to the reality of the situation. I became agreeable on the outside but resentful on the inside. And so I created confusion and pain, and was not always honest about my own feelings or needs. This unwholesome behavior due to my inner conflicts contributed to two divorces.

Using my meditation skills and directing my awareness to my feelings of unworthiness, I discovered they were just the surface of something stagnating inside—something that needed immediate attention. The feelings of inadequacy were surfacing from my unconscious mind and this unconscious material was controlling my life. (In chapter 5, I will describe how I accessed this material and what I discovered.)

There's an old cartoon that shows a caveman crafting the first wheel for his cart—but the wheels are square. In the caption he says, "Damn, it still doesn't work!" Things with sharp corners, sharp edges don't move freely. It is the same with us. Having "sharp edges" doesn't necessarily mean being aggressive; being passive can have sharp edges too. Unconscious beliefs and emotions create sharp edges in our personalities. As long as we carry suppressed unconscious beliefs and emotions as in Shishin's case, our sharp edges will keep our life from being wholesome and fulfilling.

When working with fear, for example, instead of suppressing our fear we need to be aware of what it really *feels* like. What bodily sensations are produced by fear? Can we distinguish between these visceral experiences and the stories we tell ourselves *about* our fear? By using this manual, you will begin to see the difference. We can discover that the basic experience of fear—the bodily sensations without the storyline—doesn't feel so bad. And this revelation is essential in addressing the unconscious mind and our sharp edges.

From a larger spiritual perspective, suppressing, denying, or even judging our thoughts and feelings deprives us of their guiding light. Clear awareness of mental and emotional states can illuminate our deeper unconscious realities and be a path toward inner peace, joy, and freedom.

If our life lacks joy, we must unveil the ways we block the flow of that natural energy in our body and mind. With increased awareness from a regular meditation practice, our capacity to experience joy and creativity—the natural expressions of our life force—can be realized. This book contains many personal stories of this unveiling process, including those of the authors, and presents simple steps to self-realization and healing.

What to Expect in This Book

The Great Heart Way consists of eight basic steps, compiled in the seven chapters of this book.

In chapter 1, "Recovering Creativity and Consciousness," we emphasize the mutual contributions of Western psychology and Eastern spiritual practice. From the Western perspective, we look at our "shadow" and the healing powers locked within it. We explain the relationships among the conscious, unconscious, and subconscious mind. We also consider the dangers of "spiritual bypassing," the avoidance of psychological issues in spiritual practice. We relate why the Great Heart Way of self-transformation was created and why it places so much importance on meditation.

In chapter 2, "The Royal Road to the Unconscious," we start with a short primer on how to meditate, including information on the disposition of the body, mind, and breath. We show how to deal with, and not avoid, thoughts and feelings in meditation. We finish the chapter with a discussion of the nature of self, contrasting the attachment to ego-self with the realization of True Self.

In chapter 3, "The Heart-Mind Connection," we introduce exercises designed to bring clarity to negative attitudes and patterns of behavior, such as the practices of nonjudgmental awareness and maintaining a heart-mind connection. We further explore the strong link between physical and psychological health, acknowledging the benefit of truly and deeply experiencing our feelings. The relationship between unexplored emotions and negative karma is also discussed.

In chapter 4, "The Ego's Fixed Images of Self," we learn how, at a very young age, our mind splits into conflicting concepts of good and bad, love and hate, self and other, and so on. This leads to feelings of guilt, shame, and separateness—and what we call a *fixed image,* or mental picture, of who we are. This image is supported by false beliefs and deluded attitudes of withdrawal, submission, and aggression, with which we try to fit into a world that we don't quite understand. The exercises in this chapter help us to recognize early conditioning and uncover our fixed images of self.

In chapter 5, "Releasing Fixed Images," after we discover our fixed images, we can begin to free our unconscious mind from their grip. For this we need to work directly with our thoughts and feelings. The exercises in this chapter help us to expose, "deprogram," and heal the wounds from our own fixed images.

In chapter 6, "Transforming Negative Karma," we look at the way unconscious images create negative karma in our lives and the lives of others. We will discuss how we can use this negative, destructive power in a positive and creative way through the development of nonjudgmental awareness.

In chapter 7, "The Great Heart Practice," we introduce the practice of breathing through the heart and how to maintain the heart-mind connection through our daily activities. The Dalai Lama has pointed out repeatedly that our disturbing emotions are the source of unethical conduct, suffering, and war. In this chapter, we explain that by addressing these emotions, we create inner peace which then creates outer peace. It becomes clear that war is a symptom of each individual's internal war with him or herself. We also introduce the power of praying from the heart.

How to Use This Manual

We recommend you use this manual in the following way:

- First, read the whole manual once without doing the exercises. This will give you an overall picture of the work you will be doing. At this point we also recommend you start a regular meditation practice.

• Second, we invite you read this book *again,* but this time do the exercises and begin a journal of your written responses.

• Third, repeat the series of exercises as often as you find helpful. With each iteration you will develop more awareness and go deeper into your mind. You will discover new and deeper material. And you will see your own process of transformation unfold right before your eyes.

When we started practicing this method ourselves, we realized that accessing the unconscious mind was like opening Pandora's Box: the more you open it, the more old conditioning comes rushing out. From our own experience, we can truly say this has been the most fascinating journey we have ever taken. In some ways, it reminds us of the mystery and excitement of Jules Verne's *Journey to the Center of the Earth.* The big difference is that we are going to the center of our being, to our own heart. And the only equipment we need is the light of our own awareness. We invite you to take this fascinating journey with us.

We wish you *bon voyage* on the journey of self-discovery!

1

RECOVERING CREATIVITY
AND CONSCIOUSNESS

The great error of modern psychology has been to speak of the unconscious as though it were some kind of unknowable...But insofar as the unconscious is the body...the unconscious can be known...And insofar as it is...[a] timeless principle, the unconscious can be finally realized in an act of unitive knowledge.

—ALDOUS HUXLEY[1]

One of the wonderful things about living in the twenty-first century is having unprecedented access to all the world's spiritual traditions. During the last century, spiritual leaders from Japan, Tibet, China, and Southeast Asia established meditation centers in North America and Europe and taught generations of eager students the importance of meditation. Through their efforts, and after extensive training, many Westerners like us have been sanctioned to teach Eastern meditation practices, resulting in an emergence of new ways to bring the wisdom of East and West together. The Great Heart Way combines Eastern spiritual teachings on the power of meditation with

Western psychological teachings on personal transformation, creating a holistic and eminently practical approach to one's well-being.

Through the practice of meditation, Eastern traditions emphasize our union with the Infinite Mind.[2] This Infinite Mind, which is known by different names in different cultures—God, Buddha Nature, the Divine, Allah, the Absolute, True Self, and Original Face—cannot begin to be fathomed by words. The union of the human being with the Infinite Mind is what is referred to by the phrase "transcendent experience."

This experience is available to everyone because it is always present within us, but it can only be realized through the willingness to go beyond concepts and ideas. By breaking through the boundaries of the conceptual mind, or intellect, we begin to embody a new vision of our deepest nature. This new understanding is not constricted by dualistic notions of right and wrong, life and death, self and other, young and old, healthy and sick. It is an experience of unity with all things, extending into a timeless, space-less expanse of joy and wisdom.

Through meditation we have become aware of an unconscious reality that strongly influences our conscious thoughts and behaviors. Because these unconscious processes of the mind can be difficult to access and may seem dark and intangible, we carry them as a "shadow." This shadow painfully conditions and limits our lives in myriad ways. But while the unconscious is by its nature unknown, it can be brought to the conscious mind through meditation and the development of awareness. After years of investigating and probing, Carl Jung himself concluded that meditation seems to be the "royal road to the unconscious."[3]

The Great Heart Way is a carefully considered union of spiritual development and personal transformation. Based on meditation, this method enables us to open our hearts and to bring light to the darkness of the unconscious, thereby rediscovering our full potential.

What Is the Shadow?

All of us have a hidden aspect that affects our lives without our knowledge. Some psychologists, following Jung, call this the "shadow." The shadow is like an unconscious trash bag, filled with those parts of ourselves that we've rejected. Just like our physical shadow, our unconscious shadow is always with us, whether we see it or not. As part of the Great Heart Way, you will learn to recognize and own your shadow.

We start filling this unconscious trash bag at a very early age. As young children bursting with energy, when our parents exclaim, "Can't you be quiet?" a part of us goes into the bag. To keep our parents' approval, we "bag" whatever they don't like. At school, when our teachers tell us "good children don't behave like that," we have more material for the bag. When others don't like some aspects of our personality, it too may go into the bag, and so on into adulthood.

All along the way, we learn to reject those "bagged" aspects of ourselves—even if we don't consciously know what they are. In our attempt to control others and avoid conflict and disagreement, we keep tossing in parcels. Unfortunately, every part of ourselves that we dump into the unconscious inevitably inhibits us from living a fulfilling life. Our shadow gives rise to negative projections that condition our perceptions and relationships with ourselves and the rest of the world. As physicist Fred Alan Wolf writes, "There is no 'out there' independent of what's going on 'in here.'" [4]

Through meditation, we begin to see how these negative projections work in our lives and how they affect our views of reality. Our conditioning strongly influences our perception. Consider this concrete example from the world of experimental science:

In the 1960s, English researcher Colin Blakemore and his colleagues showed that kittens reared in an environment devoid of vertical lines lost the ability to see vertical lines. They would bump into table legs, for example.

And, relatedly, in the psychological plane, as Candace Pert of the Georgetown University Medical School says, "We see what we want to believe. And we turn away from things that are too unfamiliar or unpleasant."[5]

Learning about the experiences of others can help us to uncover our own projections. Ultimately, we find we're not so different from each other, and we're not alone in dealing with our inner issues. We discover that even those things we imagine to be the worst parts of ourselves are not so unique. As one student said about his most embarrassing memory, "It would not even make the back page of the Peoria Times." Through a process of sharing, we can connect with many people going through this same process of liberation. Then, too, our struggles can become a source of inspiration for others.

In the following first-person case example, we perhaps can see some of our own struggles in a man we'll call *John*, a young professional who, by utilizing the Great Heart Way, was able to see how his negative projections were affecting his life. Details about the tools John used will follow later in this book, but here we will show an example of what it looks like to know one's shadow.

SAINT JOHN'S SHADOW

At first I observed my usual way of relating to the world. There was a constant background noise of thoughts and feelings of irritation, criticism, and anger towards others, and a basically aggressive way of dealing with my surroundings. Over the years, I had become increasingly aware of this pattern and increasingly uncomfortable with it—hence my interest in the practice.

I recognized these feelings of irritation, criticalness, and anger toward others as projections from my shadow. Then I let them be. I experienced them deeply, especially the uncomfortable body sensations, which became increasingly familiar to me as the practice went on. I was able to maintain this awareness in most of my everyday interactions, not just in meditation.

Staying present with my uncomfortable bodily sensations, I was able to access what was hidden underneath them. Some old beliefs began to surface like a bubble coming up in the mud of a swamp. All my life I believed I would fail—always. The angry, irritated thoughts were like protective armor, because not only did I believe I would fail, I was afraid to fail. To protect myself from failing, I always had to be right. My goal was to attain perfection.

Then a memory burst into my awareness: I'm about five years old and in my parents' house. My parents had decided I'd have a room all to myself, away from my sister. In the memory, I'm playing up on the third floor in this room that is now mine. I am alone, twirling a vacuum cleaner hose around my head, faster and faster. All of a sudden the metal end flies off the hose and strikes the wall, making a gaping, round hole near the foot of my bed. I don't now know why, but I am mortified by this accident. Here in the solitude of my very first own room, I've made a grievous mistake: I've soiled a secret paradise. I am afraid that I'll be condemned by my parents and lose my new room.

I told myself that no one must ever find out what I have done. The hole, itself, leads to a blackness behind the wall, where I cannot see and which seems quite mysterious. I'm at a loss as to what to do, and I'm getting desperate because sooner or later someone will come up and discover what I've done.

I have a small but fancy little picture that my parents bought for me. It shows a medieval-looking man in robes appearing quite pious and at the bottom of the picture, the title "Saint John." I go to a Catholic school and know that saints are perfect people. So I hang St. John over the offending hole. No one but me knows that my secret hides behind him.

And that's the way it's been all these years. As long as I can remember, I've been protecting myself so nobody finds out about my imperfections.

In the example of "Saint John's Shadow," we saw how John decided at a very young age to appear perfect, like Saint John, by covering his imperfections. As the years went by, John forgot about the conscious decision he'd made as a child. As an adult, he didn't know why he carried such feelings of irritation or why he always had to appear perfect. The memory of Saint John covering the hole in the wall had become part of his unconscious mind.

HEALING POWER OF THE SHADOW

One great Eastern master, Gensha, wrote over a thousand years ago that even in the dark mountain cave of demons, complete freedom is present.[6] He recognized what psychologists are now acknowledging: by entering the shadows or dark side of our personality, we can heal negative behavior patterns and emotional disturbances at their root. Complete freedom is present wherever and whenever we abide in the clarity of our nonjudgmental awareness. Otherwise we only see the gloom and doom of the shadows.

It's important to clarify what we mean when we talk about the dark side of our personality. This is not a horror story. The terms "dark side" or "shadow side" are not judgmental or pejorative. The unconscious is referred to in these terms only because it exists in the absence of light. It is unilluminated and unseen. In our conscious mind, we have the light of awareness. Until we develop awareness of our unconscious mind, that side of our mind is in the dark. That's all! The dark side isn't like the evil side in *Star Wars,* something to be assiduously avoided. On the contrary, through the Great Heart Way we can come to realize that it is a source of true goodness and healing.

PROJECTIONS OF THE SHADOW

There is a connection between our shadow and the energy we project into the world through our attitudes and actions. Our view of the world and other people depends on the size of the shadow-bag we're dragging behind us, and what we're carrying in it. An old Zen story illustrates this point clearly.

> There was a traveling monk who went from temple to temple carrying a big bag of horse manure over his shoulder. When he arrived at a new temple, he would set his bag down and exclaim, "This place smells like shit!" Then he'd pick up his bag and move on to the next temple and do the same thing, surprised every time.

Like the monk in this story, we are ignorant of what we're carrying in our bag—we are unconsciously projecting it onto everybody and everything, and it forms our perception of the world.

Another analogy we could use for the dark side of the personality is a film canister.[7] We keep putting the rejected parts of ourselves into the canister, then the film is unconsciously projected onto the world through our thoughts, words, and actions. A person's anger could be rolled up inside the canister and then brought out unexpectedly and projected on the face of another. These projections dissipate our energy and obscure our clarity. The more we put into our "canister," the less energy we have for creative and spiritual purposes.

So how do we recognize the existence of our shadow? We get hints about its contents when we notice who we irrationally hate or harbor negative feelings toward.

Consider this example: Andrea lives in a small town in Minnesota. Another woman, Roberta, just moved into her apartment building. Andrea thinks that Roberta is too sexy, and she finds herself obsessing about Roberta. This is a clue from her subconscious mind that she has suppressed sexual feelings. These denied feelings are being projected onto Roberta. So we must notice precisely whom we hate or get obsessed with. We sometimes even get entangled with virtual strangers when we're particularly sensitive to a quality in them that we've rejected in ourselves.

Theologian Miceal Ledwith offers this observation in *What the Bleep Do We Know!?*:

> *We are creating our own reality every day, though we find that very hard to accept—there is nothing more exquisitely pleasant than to blame somebody else for the way we are. It's his fault or is her fault; it's the system; it's God, it's my parents…Whatever way we observe the world around us is what comes back to us, and the reason why my life, for instance, is so lacking in joy and happiness and fulfillment is because my focus is lacking in those same things exactly.*

In John's case earlier—having decided at a young age he had to appear perfect and hide his imperfections behind Saint John—he couldn't accept imperfection in anyone else. Noticing his irritation toward others' shortcomings was his clue that he had condemned imperfection in himself.

The Great Heart Way is a path of attention and awareness. On this path, we begin to notice where we project our hatred, and with whom we become obsessed. These clues help us recognize what we're carrying in our shadow. They are flashes of light in this darkness, showing us that our shadow contains none other than our own severed life force. To reclaim our shadow is to recover our birthright.

Imagine the energy John wasted feeling angry and irritated at the world. Do you recognize this loss in yourself? What if you were able to free all the energy now caught up in negativity, making it available for creative and life-affirming actions and relationships? Who wouldn't like to have more energy available? On the Great Heart Way of transformation, your shadow is the source of this additional energy! We expend much effort trying to hide our shadow, bound up in guilt and shame. When we release that energy, it becomes available to us for other purposes. The energy was always there, we just couldn't access it. As a Zen verse says: "Don't foolishly look here and there. If you keep asking, 'What is my True Self?' it is like pleading innocent while clutching the stolen goods."[8]

Many of us view ourselves and the world as fragmented and incomplete. Trying to protect ourselves from being hurt when we were kids, we built all kinds of defense mechanisms that acted like protective walls and separated us from the rest of the world. As adults if we do not work at dissolving these defense mechanisms and healing the old hurts, we will have a distorted view of the world, a view grounded in ignorance. And this inaccurate view of reality is actually quite dangerous. It's like a blindfolded captain navigating a large ship through the ice-fields in the North Sea—doomed to disaster.

We simply can't avoid life's dangers if we don't see clearly. When our view of the world is blocked by our own shadow, we stumble everywhere: in our jobs, in our relationships, and worst of all in relation to ourselves. John's view of an imperfect world prevented him from being relaxed and happy, and from developing deep relationships with his family and his colleagues at work.

To take the veil of delusion from our eyes, we must first recognize that the veil *exists*. Then, with all of our heart, we must desire to remove it. The process of unveiling can be done by *anyone* who sincerely wants to do so.

The practices of the Great Heart Way train us to recover our bound-up energy. And they allow us to experience, in our own body and mind, that the world is not fragmented. We can experience for ourselves that we are an intrinsic manifestation of a unified universe.

Dr. Stanislav Grof, the founder of Transpersonal Psychology wrote:

> *The deepest nature of humanity is not bestial, but divine. The universe is imbued with creative intelligence and consciousness is inextricably woven into its fabric. Our identification with the separate body-ego is an illusion and our true identity is the totality of existence. This understanding provides a natural basis for reverence for life, cooperation and synergy, concerns for humanity and the planet as a whole, and deep ecological awareness.*[9]

THE GATEWAY TO THE UNCONSCIOUS MIND

Most of us are only familiar with our mind's most obvious aspect: the intellect. The intellect, with its dualistic understanding of things, is the mind that solves many of the everyday problems in the world: building a ship, passing a test, learning a language. Much of Western philosophy and knowledge is based on the Cartesian ideal, "I think therefore I am." And "thinking" is the word that describes what the intellect does. Yet this approach, equating the whole of our being with our thinking, ignores the rest of the vast spectrum of human experience. It ignores altogether our spiritual and emotional reality. There is nothing wrong with an intellectual way of relating to the world, but it is important to realize that it is somewhat one-dimensional. There is much more to our mind and world, and it would be a pity to spend a lifetime without plumbing the endless depths of our treasures.

There is a Buddhist parable[10] about two friends, a rich man and a poor man, who were drinking together one night. Toward the end of the evening, the poor man falls asleep and the rich man must leave the next day on a long trip. Concerned for his friend, the rich man takes a precious gem and hides it in the lining of the poor man's jacket; when he awakes, he can sell it and live in luxury for the rest of his life. The poor man, however, never discovers the gem. He spends years in poverty, barely able to survive. When the rich friend returns, he is shocked. Revealing the gem to his friend, he says, "I had already provided for you. You were wealthy all this time and never noticed." Unless we know we have a treasure within us, we will never find it.

Where is the treasure? One important answer is that it is stored in our unconscious mind.[11]

As spiritual teachers, our knowledge of the unconscious mind is primarily experiential. Just as it would be difficult to describe the taste of water to someone who has never drunk it, it's impossible to explain the unconscious mind to someone who has never experienced it. Even in modern psychology, there is confusion about the exact meaning of the term "unconscious." Many of the discussions are speculative. General descriptions fail to convey enough information, while specific descriptions can still exclude aspects that are important. Experiential understanding is the key. When asked to define pornography, Justice Potter Stewart famously said, "I know it when I see it."[12] As spiritual guides we could say the same regarding the unconscious: "We know it when we see it."

Within the context of the Great Heart Way, we like to use the following definitions: The conscious mind is everything we are aware of—everything we hear, see, feel, taste, smell, and think—and all our explicit notions about ourselves, others, and the world. The unconscious mind is everything we're not aware of, including everything we don't know about ourselves, our projections, the world, and reality.

The *sub*conscious mind is the stage in between the conscious and unconscious mind. In the subconscious, we are not completely aware of
our mind's contents—nor are we completely unaware of them. Subtle
thoughts, feelings, and dreams emanate from the unconscious to become partially conscious in the subconscious. Thus the subconscious
mind is the gateway to the unconscious mind.

SPIRITUAL BYPASSING

Spiritual practice in America today is quite different from traditional
spiritual practice in the East. There it was mostly relegated to the do-
main of solitary monks, who usually did not deal with the shadow aspects of their personalities, and because of the nature of monastic
living, many of them never needed to. Yet overlooking these dark aspects of personality has negative consequences. Psychologist John
Welwood calls this tendency "spiritual bypassing."[13] When spiritual
practice is used to avoid or bypass the personal shadow, it may momentarily transcend the shadow's effects; but sooner or later, the
shadow will cloud these temporary insights. And spiritual bypassing
will manifest as spiritual sickness.

Most of us have witnessed the monstrous consequences of spiritual sickness, which is as common in the West as in the East. Substance abuse, sexual promiscuity, and child molestation among
spiritual leaders of all denominations are direct results of spiritual
bypassing. But these are extreme examples and there are many examples where the effects of spiritual bypassing might not be so ap-
parent. At our Center, there are students who are passive-aggressive
and hypocritical. Others try to be perfect by denying their shadows.
Unless they deal with their inner issues, they will not be empowered
to teach at our Center. However, there are spiritual leaders who have
never worked on their shadows and have never been involved in any
scandals—but these leaders tend to show a lack of heart and rigid,

inflexible behavior. In his book *Joy,* psychotherapist Alexander Lowen says:

> *Some regard their rigidity as a sign of strength, as proof that they can stand up to adversity, that they will not yield or break under stress, that they can tolerate discomfort even distress. I believe we have become a nation of survivors so frightened of illness and death that we are unable to live as free people.*

When we avoid the conflicting aspects of our personalities, we become more entangled in their web.

Most of the spiritual leaders from the East were trained in an environment absent of the opposite sex and the complications of livelihood and family life. Many were not prepared to deal with the complications of modern life in the West. America's spiritual practice is growing among lay people, both men and women, who have jobs, families, and relationships. The traditional Eastern monastic model of spiritual practice neither wholly reaches nor wholly satisfies the needs of the Western lay community.

Lay life can be enriched by spiritual practice and spiritual practice can be enriched by lay life. If spiritual practice does not engage with the richness of relationships and the pressures of society, it can become arid and irrelevant. On the other hand, personal life can benefit considerably from the expansiveness of spiritual practice, without which everyday life can become narrow and oppressive.

The Importance of Meditation

In our education system we are not offered any real guidance for working with the mind. Confusing the mind with the intellect, we are filled up with all kind of ideas, concepts, and general knowledge. While it is very important for success in the material world, rational thought doesn't touch the depth of the mind, which can only be experienced and not thought about. To experience the depth of our mind is to realize who we truly are. It is to realize our divine origin. It's realizing the meaning of our life on this planet and, ultimately, the love, peace, and joy we can extend to the world. This is not to say we shouldn't develop our intellect or endeavor to be successful in the material world, only that we must develop our mind's awareness as well.

The "royal road" to understanding the depth of our mind is meditation. Meditation is not about withdrawing from the world or just sitting around doing nothing. Meditation is a practice of learning to see ourselves more clearly. And this in turn leads to true acts of compassion and empathy. Moreover, some of the greatest discoveries and creative acts—including those of science, politics, and art—had their origins in the minds of meditators.[14] This ability to maintain awareness and be present is essential to any serious pursuit. Thus meditation has tremendous social benefits—not just for the individual but also for the world. And, after all, the truth is that the two are not really separate.

UNTYING THE INVISIBLE ROPES OF CONDITIONING

We live in a dualistic world that teaches us to identify with some aspects of our mind and reject others. The speed and complexity of modern life make it difficult to slow down and see what's going on around and inside of us. Society teaches us that we are separate; television, radio, and newspapers reinforce this illusion, encouraging us to build walls around our hearts. We grow up as alienated beings who are trapped inside the illusory reality produced by our own minds. This is like being caught inside a computer-generated virtual reality, unaware that what we experience is not what actually exists.

All of us carry conditioned beliefs and prejudices in our minds that bind us with invisible ropes. Often these beliefs are the cause of our discomfort and unhappiness. Yet we continue to carry them because we are not aware of how they affect us. Nor are we aware of how to function in life without them. We would rather be miserable with the life we know than make the effort to create a boundless, but unfamiliar, new life.

I (Shishin) worked with Professor John Isaacs at the University of California who would say that "there is no tyranny as great as the tyranny of the first successful solution."[15] Our childhood strategies did serve us when we were vulnerable and in need of safety, protection, and our parents' love. As adults we unconsciously hold on to these strategies, even though they're no longer valid or useful, even though they cause us much suffering. But difficulties that touch us deeply enough can rouse us to look into our mind and approach life in a new way. Then difficulty becomes an opportunity for awakening and for living with compassion, humor, patience, joy, courage, and empathy. Meditation can help us to achieve this.

The thirteenth-century Zen master Eihei Dogen said, "To practice meditation is to study the self."[16] The Great Heart Way takes this thoroughly to heart, and to take full advantage of the processes in this book, you will need to develop a consistent meditation practice.

All major spiritual traditions encourage meditation, contemplation, or prayer to clarify and connect with unconscious aspects of ourselves. The basis of these disciplines is quieting and focusing the mind. In meditation, we learn to watch our thoughts and feelings without judging or evaluating them. This is the most effective way to get to know ourselves at the most intimate level.

People come to meditation for a wide variety of reasons, all of which are, of course, valid; but the masters come to meditation to get in touch with their Infinite Mind and to actualize that Mind in their daily life. Through meditation we can not only discover the activity of our own mind, we can open up to a life full of possibilities.

Realizing Your Pumpkin Nature

There is a Japanese children's story about pumpkins in a temple garden. The pumpkins were arguing about who was the best: the roundest, largest, the orangest, and so on. They were making such a clamor that they roused the temple priest, who came to see what was going on. The priest sized up the situation and told all of the pumpkins to put their "hands" on the top of their "heads" and tell him what they noticed. Immediately they noticed that they were all attached by the same vine, that in essence they were one body. They were the same. Spiritual masters have been teaching this same truth for centuries. Much of our suffering and inner anguish will naturally vanish when we intimately realize for ourselves that we are one with all things. But this intimate realization cannot be done with the intellect alone.

Self-centered thoughts actually separate us from fully experiencing each moment. They are based on protecting our self-image rather than on engaging each moment as it occurs. When we carefully reflect on our thoughts, we notice that a thought arises, persists, and passes away. Then another thought arises, persists, and passes away. Still we might think: "This is important! This is real!" But each moment we can bring our attention back to the present, without judging, criticizing, or evaluating. In the practice of meditation, we begin to see the nature of our thoughts. The more we are able to let go of our self-centered thoughts, the more we are able to let go of our protective shield, and the more truth will shine through our life.

To experience freedom and awakening, we need to get in touch with the spaciousness of our being, which is pure awareness. Awareness is cultivated in meditation. Then, like the vast sky, we can contain our beliefs, projections, fixations, and compulsions without acting on them or judging them. As the physicist Heisenberg observed, the experimenter modifies the results of the experiment.[17] In the same way, pure awareness of all aspects of our personality serves to modify and transform them.

AWARENESS, COURAGE, AND COMPASSION

In order to transform troublesome behavior patterns, we need to cultivate awareness, courage, and compassion through the practice of meditation. In meditation, we learn to see the way thoughts arise in the larger space of awareness, which is much greater than any thought. With no qualities of good or bad, awareness expands the context of our life in a way that allows us to witness our perceived problems without judgment.

From awareness arises the courage of an open heart. It takes courage to be willing to open our heart, even to situations that are difficult or painful. And it takes courage to trust this raw experience and accept it for what it is. This means letting down our protective shields and allowing events and people in. The courage of awareness with an open heart manifests as true compassion. Antoine de Saint-Exupéry, the French aviator and writer of the twentieth century wrote, "It is only with the heart that one can see rightly; what is essential is invisible to the eye."[18]

True compassion is an unconditional acceptance of ourselves and others. In the Great Heart, we cultivate this kind of compassion in order to learn from our problems and mistakes. Through meditation we learn to be unconditionally present with our life, just as it is, without needing to make up stories to suppress our real experience. People in many disciplines are now beginning to recognize the healing power of this unconditional presence.[19]

When we start a meditation practice we start a vertical journey into the depth of the mind. We then begin to experience that there is much more to the mind, a new and infinite dimension that is beyond reason and intellectual understanding. Beyond our narrow, limited versions of "self," we experience a new, healthier version of who we truly are. This new version is not limited by fear, guilt, or hatred. It is

not bounded by conventional notions of space and time. Nor is it limited by conventional knowledge and understanding.

Human beings are naturally afraid of the unknown. And by extension we're afraid of the unknown part of our own mind, which is like
a darkened house. Meditation allows us to explore that house. It provides us with a torch that dispels the terrifying shadows and illuminates mind's inherent treasures. So don't be afraid. This process is safe.

2

THE ROYAL ROAD
TO THE UNCONSCIOUS

Meditation…seems to be a royal road to the unconscious.

—C.G. JUNG[1]

HOW TO MEDITATE

This chapter focuses on the basics of meditation. The first aim of meditation is to discipline the mind so it stops jumping from thought to thought, like a wild monkey jumping from branch to branch. The exercises presented in later chapters show how to use meditation to get in touch with unfelt feelings, hidden images and beliefs, and other forms of conditioning.

There are three aspects of meditation: the disposition of the body, disposition of the mind, and attention to breathing. We will present the essential points here. For further details, you can consult one of the excellent books on meditation, such as *Zen Meditation in Plain English* by John Daishin Buksbazen.

THE BODY IN MEDITATION

The way we hold our body reflects our internal state. If the shoulders are rounded and protrude forward, it could be a protective stance. If the body is rigid, it could be a symptom of an inflexible mind. The body needs to be stable and relaxed in order for the breath to flow freely and the mind to settle down.

For meditation practice, we recommend sitting on a round cushion on the floor, preferably on a carpet or a large square flat cushion. The body weight should be centered at a point a few inches below the navel and in the center of the body. This is called the *hara* in Japanese. It is the center of the energy and gravity in our body.

Form a stable base with the legs in a cross-legged manner or with the legs bent back under the buttocks. For examples of various postures refer to the illustrations. Hold the spine straight with the head erect. The nose should be over the navel, and the ears should be over

Full Lotus leg position

Half Lotus leg position

Burmese leg position

the shoulders. The eyes are kept open but lowered. If you close your eyes, there is a tendency to fall asleep.

Physical tension disturbs our mental stability, not only during meditation but in life in general. If the head or the chin projects forward, there is pressure on the neck. This affects the nerves in the spinal column and thus stimulates thoughts and pain.

If a permanent injury or physical problem makes it too painful to sit cross-legged on the floor, you can sit on your heels with your legs beneath you, either on a cushion or on a meditation bench; or you can sit in a chair. If you sit in a chair, keep your back straight and your feet flat on the floor. Do not lean backwards or abnormally curve your spine.

In some meditation traditions, students are instructed to find a posture that allows them to be unaware of the body. They may then slump over or lean against the wall. While it is better to meditate with poor posture than not to meditate at all, sitting straight with a stable base makes it is easier to discipline the mind.

If pain in your legs or back becomes intense, try another leg position, or shift your leg positions between one meditation period and another. Quite often, meditators will fidget and continuously adjust their bodies. This behavior could be a sign that that person is uncomfortable just being with themselves. When the urge to fidget arises, just notice it and let it go. The same principle applies if the desire to scratch an itch arises: don't scratch it, and see what happens. There's an expression that a snake doesn't know its own shape until it's confined to a bamboo tube. In the same way, we might not get to know ourselves until we discipline ourselves to sit still and watch the activity of our body and mind.

You can place your hands in your lap or on your knees. There are a number of traditional hand positions. In the most common one, the hands are held against the lower abdomen with left hand on top of the right one and the middle knuckles of each hand touching. The ends of the thumbs are lightly brought together so that the thumbs and the rest of the hands form an oval. The position of the thumbs can be an indicator of the activity of the mind. If you press the thumbs tightly together, your mind is too taut. If the thumbs droop or drop down, your mind is wandering. Like a string instrument, the mind needs to be in tune with the body—neither too tight nor too loose.

Legs bent back under the buttocks

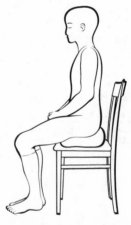

Meditating on a chair

MEDITATION AND THE BREATH

Breathing should be natural. Although sometimes, when we start to pay attention to our breath, it seems unnatural. When you breathe in, the abdomen naturally rises and when you breathe out, it falls. Some people get confused and do the opposite when they start paying attention to their breath. Don't push the air into your abdomen; just expand the lower abdomen and chest.

There is a story about a man with a long beard, who was asked if he slept with his beard over or under the covers. He admitted that he did not know. That night he put his beard over the covers. But that didn't feel right. So he put his beard under the covers. That didn't feel right either. He spent all night moving his beard under and over the covers—and didn't get a moment of sleep.

When you first pay attention to your breath, you might find it feels very unnatural, but it will settle down. You will find that your breathing will slow from about fifteen cycles per minute to about five or six cycles per minute. When you breathe freely and unrestrictedly, the energy can flow through your body and consequently reduce your level of anxiety.

THE MIND IN MEDITATION

Initially, the best way to discipline the mind is to focus your attention on the breath. Put your mind's eye in the lower abdomen, and silently count the inhalations and the exhalations from one to ten. Then start over again. If you lose track and your mind starts to wander, return to one and start over again. If you find that you are counting higher than ten, start over again. There is nothing magical about the number ten; it is simply not too small to give us false assurance and not too large to generate disinterest and boredom.

When you put all your attention and energy into counting the numbers of breaths, extraneous thoughts cannot arise. On the exhalation, your whole body and mind is concentrated on the sound of the number one: *"wooooooooooooooooon."* On the inhalation, your whole body and mind concentrate on the sound of the number two: *"tooooooooooooooooooooo."* Pay close attention to the point of transition between inhaling and exhaling. This is where mind's concentration is weakest. Just as in martial arts, the point of weakest attention is when your opponent just finishes exhaling. This is the best time to attack. In meditation, it is the best time to pay close attention to your mind.

The point here is not whether you can count from one to ten without a miss; the point is to discipline the mind so that, more and more, you can maintain your attention in the present moment without fantasizing about the future or reminiscing about the past. Then eventually you will be able to maintain a non-judging mind, a mind that just observes what is so, without prejudice. In later chapters, we will talk about focusing on bodily sensations and feelings in order to access the unconscious mind. But first you must learn to hold your mind steady and not chase after thoughts.

When you grab onto one thought, another thought will arise to take its place. Then you grab onto that one, too. This chasing process continues indefinitely. There is no relief and there is no end. In meditation, you learn how to hold your mind like the great sky, which allows the clouds to drift by without trying to hold onto them or follow them.

A sound meditative technique is to use something simple and ordinary, such as the breath. In order to explore our mind through meditation, we have to be patient and steady. We can't just fly directly to the center of profound experiences. We have to go on foot. Besides, by flying over our inner terrain, we will never learn the way to the heart of the unconscious. So keep it simple, keep your attention on the breath. Your breathing does not need to be associated with any kind of *thoughts*—because conceptual thinking cannot reach the precision required in meditation.

Sitting meditation is one form of practice. We can also meditate while walking, chanting, speaking, eating, and resting. When walking, either focus on your breath or on the soles of your feet and maintain nonjudgmental awareness. When eating, focus your attention on the act of eating and use your breath to sustain your mindfulness. Similarly you can cultivate mindfulness in all of your other activities

Before starting to practice meditation, most of us can't separate delusion from truth. We're like the foolish farmer who keeps chickens in his yard and goes around collecting chicken shit instead of eggs—and then wonders why the omelets don't taste so good. By learning to pay attention, we don't keep making that mistake. And with total mindfulness, we don't keep worrying about how we should *be*. All things will naturally unfold: our life, our careers, our relationships.

SHOULD AND COULD

There is an ancient tale of Mr. Sei who lived in a small village with his horse.[2] Because he had a horse, Mr. Sei was one of the wealthiest villagers. His neighbors would come to him and tell him how lucky he was to have that horse. Now he could plow a much larger field, have a much larger income, and take much better care of his family. But Mr. Sei was a wise man. He didn't say anything, he just nodded his head.

One day the horse ran away. Then Mr. Sei's neighbors came and told him how unlucky he was that his horse ran away. Mr. Sei said nothing. Not commenting, he just nodded his head in acknowledgment of the situation. Then the horse returned—followed by a second horse. Mr. Sei's neighbors came to say how lucky he was that his horse ran away. Now he had two horses. Again Mr. Sei said nothing and simply nodded his head, acknowledging the state of things.

Meanwhile, his son was plowing the field with the second horse, and he had an accident and broke his leg. The neighbors came to tell Mr. Sei how unlucky he was to have that second horse. His son broke his leg and couldn't help in the fields.

Then a war broke out in the province and the lords conscripted all the young men to fight. But Mr. Sei's son had a broken leg and couldn't go into battle. So the neighbors came to tell Mr. Sei how lucky he was that his son broke his leg....

And so it goes. We have so many ideas about how things should or could be. The truth is that we never know how things will turn out. True freedom is found in just taking things as they are. When practicing meditation, look into your own mind and body without judging. Just be attentive. When physical or psychological pain arises, allow it to be there. Without criticizing or condemning it, be totally present with the pain. Eventually it will give you insight into your basic ground of being.

Dealing with Thoughts in Meditation

You may be wondering, "What is the best way to quiet the mind during meditation?" It's not really a matter of *quieting* the mind per se; rather, it's a matter of bringing our attention back to the breath whenever it has begun to move anywhere else. When the mind is active, just return your attention to breathing in and breathing out. You don't have to worry about the thoughts; they will take care of themselves. Trying to push them away is just the flip-side of grabbing onto thoughts. Instead, return your mind gently but firmly to counting your breaths. If you have to do this over and over and over again, that's okay. The point is to learn how to live in each moment, to be totally absorbed in each moment, with no separation from that moment. Little by little—by concentrating on your breathing and focusing your attention—the mind and the body will settle down.

Consider this instruction by a seventeenth-century meditation master:

As long as you deliberately try to stop your rising thoughts, the thought of trying to stop them wars against the continually arising thought and there is no end to it.... "Well," you may wonder, "then what can I do to stop them?" Even if, despite yourself, thoughts of clinging and craving arise, just let them come, don't develop them any further, don't attach to them and don't identify yourself with them. Without concerning yourself about whether to stop your rising thoughts or not to stop them, just don't bother with them and return to your counting. Then there is nothing else they can do but vanish. When there's no one there to fight with, things can't help but simply come to an end of themselves.[3]

Meditation practice is not like fast food service: it doesn't yield immediate results. The one essential ingredient is patience. And the secret to the practice is to continue under all circumstances: pleasant or unpleasant, encouraging or discouraging. Children would never succeed in learning to walk if they had any idea of what it meant to fail and were fearful of it. They may fall and hit the floor hard, and they may cry for a while. Then they get up and do it again. This is a wonderful lesson to learn from toddlers: don't give up.

Ancient wisdom tells us that one thousand failures become one success. Without those one thousand failures, there would be no success. And Einstein said, "In order to be successful, the scientist has to be willing to grope in the dark for many years."[4] We, too, must be willing to be foiled at every turn.

Meditative awareness brings peace and freedom beyond the confusion of likes and dislikes. One ancient teacher said, "If you wish to see the truth, then hold no opinions for or against. The struggle between what one likes and what one dislikes is the disease of the mind."[5] If there is judgment in meditation, a unified life of true peace is as distant as heaven from earth.

Thoughts come and go like clouds in the sky: their nature is to arise, dwell, and then decay. How can we possibly identify with the nature or quality of our thoughts? Our thoughts are not who we are. In fact, our thoughts do not even reflect reality. Boundless peace—perfect and all-pervading—is reached by letting go of those thoughts.

DEALING WITH FEELINGS IN MEDITATION

In traditional Zen meditation, feelings are handled in a fashion similar to thoughts. The meditator is instructed not to engage them, and reminded that of their own accord all feelings and states of mind will pass. In the Great Heart Way, it is essential to learn how to just feel emotions without rationalizing or explaining them. It is also very important that we do not try to find a "solution" that will make the feelings disappear. Do a body scan and identify the nature and location of the feelings. Breathe gently through your heart into the areas where the feelings manifest. Let the sensation permeate through your body and just experience it without judging.

We create all kinds of illusions in our own minds. We create good and evil, enlightenment and delusion—none of which have any substance. We create fears and all kinds of projections about our fears. And then we rationalize and justify these fears. The point is that our brain—which provides us with rational thoughts so useful for problem solving—can be easily fooled. Very easily. Again, in meditation we learn to just feel the emotions that come up, without acting on them or judging them.

FALSE VIEWS OF THE SELF

The Buddha taught that if we can let go of our false views of self, we can realize enlightenment. The esoteric teachings of all religions point to the enlightened potential within all of us. In Luke 17:21, Jesus said, "The Kingdom of God is within you." But when we cling to habitual ways of behaving based on false beliefs, all of our actions project an erroneous view of self. Letting go of these false views opens us to the enlightened life.

The purpose of meditation is to experience the interconnectedness of all things. As long as we believe that we are separate from everyone and everything else, we will behave in ways that aggrandize ourselves at the expense of others. This attitude leads to unhealthy ways to resolve conflicts and leads to war. As Stanislav Grof wrote: "Those who initiate war activities are typically substituting external targets for elements in their own psyches that should be properly faced in personal exploration."[6]

When the Buddha awakened and attained the enlightened state, he realized there is no self that we can positively grab hold of and say, "This is it!" We all act as if we have a lasting, independent, and separate self. It's a habit that most of us don't question or explain. Fostering and protecting this self is our constant preoccupation—and this, as the Buddha taught, is the cause of all of our suffering. All loss and gain, all pleasure and pain arise because we identify with this vague feeling of an independent self and are so emotionally attached and involved with it, we accept it unquestioningly. The Buddha taught that the path to happiness and freedom—as hard as it may be to believe—is to realize that ultimately there is no ego-self.

Now you may ask, "If there is no independent self, how do we function?" When we're totally absorbed in some activity, we forget the ego-self. The best athletes, musicians, and artists don't think about what they are doing when they're doing it. When they practice long and hard enough, they don't need to think in order to perform. Imagine what would happen to a platform diver if she started thinking about what to do next, just as she left the platform. Think about how a good football quarterback knows to avoid a rush from his blind side, or how a great point guard in basketball can deliver a no-look pass right on target. By letting go of attachment to a limited, ego-grasping self, they expand their consciousness to include the entire field of play. Imagine if they could expand that consciousness to the entire globe.

EXPERIENCE OF NO EGO-SELF

In the last century, the brilliant theoretical physicist Erwin Schrödinger turned his thoughts to philosophical questions. He is one of the deepest philosophical thinkers of all the physicists who brought us quantum physics. He wrote: "The reason why our sentient, percipient, and thinking ego is met nowhere within our scientific world picture can easily be indicated in seven words, *because it is itself the world picture.* It is identical with the whole and therefore cannot be contained in it as part of it."[7] That is exactly what the Buddha said 500 years BCE.

It is impossible to experience no ego-self and manifest this experience in our life when our life is bound by unconscious fixed images that result in constricted and destructive attitudes. Releasing those images is an important step on the spiritual path. When we're no longer carrying those unconscious beliefs, life becomes simpler, more joyful, and healthier. Our divine origins and our infinite life open up to us.

By just staying with the pain associated with our unconscious images without avoiding or repressing it, we expand our consciousness. An ancient Zen master once said that "without the bitter cold that penetrates to the bone, the plum blossoms could not bloom in the spring."[8]

The path of transmuting the energy of emotions into compassionate clarity must rest on a firm foundation of meditation practice. Meditation teaches us just to be. Most of us do everything we can to avoid this. When we're left alone with our own experience, we become very nervous and start thinking about what we should be doing or feeling.

The discipline of Great Heart practice can help you transform old disturbing emotions into the wisdom of seeing things as they are. It will allow you to stop manipulating your experience so that it measures up to the false standards you might have created. By freeing yourself from the grip of the narrow ego, you will be able to distinguish your actual feelings from the stories you might tell yourself.

Stories are mental fabrications, judgments or interpretations of our experience. We use our stories to draw conclusions about who we are and to feel in control. Usually we're not even aware of the stories. Unconsciously we come to believe they are an accurate portrayal of reality, but meditation helps us see through them by cultivating awareness. Returning to our breath time after time, we can see our tendency of getting attached to the stories, and we can recognize that our egos use them to limit the experience of who we are.

The first instruction in meditation is to focus your mind on your breathing. When you first start doing this you might say to yourself, "What the Buddha taught about no-self is not true." All you can see is a determined egomaniac trying to get your attention away from following your breath. That maniac in your mind uses all manner of distractions to insure its perpetuation. It would rather think about things that are terrible and horrible than be constrained to counting the breath. The journey to "no-ego-self" begins when we notice that all of our mental activity is designed to protect our self-image from any intrusion. The ego feels safe as long as you do not question its reality. The ego says, why be happy when we are safe with our unhappiness? Why feel good when we are comfortable with our misery? Why practice meditation and discipline the mind when we can let our mind be unruly like wild monkeys?

Some people find safety in misery; some find safety in aggrandizing themselves; some find safety in their bad habits. We cling to whatever maintains our separate sense of self. The ego has its own survival mechanisms. The more we meditate, the more we notice how the ego tries to preserve itself. And we start to see little gaps between the thoughts.

As Zen Master Dogen wrote: "To study the self is to forget the self."[9] Ultimately, there is no ego-self.

LOOKING FOR TRUTH

We all tend to look for some truth to believe in and follow religiously. But one great mystic advises us not to seek for the truth, only to cease to cherish our opinions.[10] To seek "truth" is to look for something outside of ourselves. And our "opinions" unfortunately only bind us tighter to our pain and suffering. Every opinion is just another way to protect, aggrandize, and perpetuate our "ego-self." As long as we're looking for truth from the outside, we will never realize happiness, satisfaction, joy, and freedom.

Most of us fall into the trap of critically judging ourselves when we don't meet our own standards. These standards are some kind of ideal we have, which has nothing to do with reality. Be who you are! Don't try to be some idea of who you think you should be. In order to reveal who we truly are we need to have a trusting mind. Through meditation—by being in each moment without pondering the future or past—we raise the trusting mind. Then we have the confidence to let go of cherished opinions.

Letting go of cherished opinions, our boundless, divine origin is naturally revealed. When who we are is revealed, this strengthens our trusting mind, which allows us to release more cherished opinions, until everything is revealed as a manifestation of truth.

There was a popular comic book character called the Silver Surfer. His body was like mercury, and he rode around the cosmos on a surfboard. In one episode, he was looking for truth. You followed him as he surfed through the galaxies and universes. Then, of course, in the last frame he finally finds it. Looking down, he notices that his surfboard is in the very place where he started. That is what our journey is about: realizing our true home. This is the real journey we make in meditation.

You can start meditating on your own. It is important to be regular in your practice. Begin by meditating ten or fifteen minutes a day. This way you will not set any goals that you cannot accomplish. Gradually lengthen the time to perhaps thirty minutes a day. Find a quiet time and place. If you want to deepen your meditation, you will eventually have to find a teacher and a meditation center where you can practice. Some people are more vigorous than others in pursuing this journey. It is easy to go astray, and a good teacher can help you keep focused and on track. There are meditation traditions in all religions, and centers can easily be located through the Internet or publications that emphasize meditation.

3

THE HEART–MIND CONNECTION

Perhaps everything that frightens us is, in its deepest essence, something helpless that needs our love.

—RAINIER MARIA RILKE[1]

I n Western culture, emotions are generally viewed with suspicion. Some people treat them as alien objects to be avoided, while others are completely overwhelmed by their emotions and uncontrollably act them out. The Great Heart Way teaches neither of these approaches. Those in the first category repress their emotions. Those in the second category also avoid feeling their emotions. By acting them out, they do not get in touch with the deeper reality that underlies surface emotions such as anger, jealousy, or envy. In fact, there are many misconceptions about what feelings actually are. This is because most of us like to *think* about feelings but are unwilling to start feeling them. Why is this? To drop into our feelings without holding back anything requires us to drop into the unknown. Dropping into feelings and the unconscious go hand in hand—and conceptual thinking cannot go there.

Aldous Huxley[2] said that the unconscious is the body, which can be realized through *unitive* knowing. Feelings are not only the language of the body, but since the body is the unconscious, they are also the language of the unconscious mind. To see our emotions as alien, "other," or separate from us, harms our physical bodies. The key to health and healing is to learn the language of the body, in other words, to learn how to feel. Alexander Lowen writes:

> *Freedom is the absence of restraint to the flow of feeling, grace is the expression of this flow in movement while beauty is the manifestation of the inner harmony such a flow engenders. They denote a healthy body and therefore, a healthy mind.[3]*

Psychologist John Welwood notes that the subject of emotions is still very confusing for Western psychology. While many psychologists would agree in private about the role of love in the healing process, the words "love" and "heart" are not only absent in the therapeutic literature, but also the literature itself lacks heart. He writes:

> *Western psychology had not provided me with an understanding of heart…It was only in turning to the meditative traditions that I came to appreciate the unconditional goodness at the core of being human, and this in return helped me to understand the possibility of unconditional love and its role in the healing process.[4]*

The fear of emotions is symptomatic of how alienated we have become from ourselves. According to the Christian mystic Meister Eckhart, the reason man does not know himself is due to the layers of protection he has built around his heart.[5] The Dalai Lama and other

Tibetan teachers speak of their great surprise and shock when they discovered how much self-hatred Westerners feel.[6]

Such intense self-hatred and blame is not found in traditional Buddhist cultures or in many indigenous people, where the true mind is the heart-mind. If you ask a Tibetan Buddhist monk about his mind, he points to his heart. In this tradition, the heart and mind are one reality, one heart-mind. A person whose mind is grounded in the heart possesses a compassionate clarity in tune with reality. Our True Self manifests through an open heart while the ego manifests through the head. When we connect our heads with our hearts, our egotistical tendencies are filtered out by the heart. Unconditional love is the trademark of the True Self while fear is the trademark of the ego. The realization of heart-mind does not include the ego-grasping ignorance that is the basis of self-hatred. Ego-grasping and its relation to emotional states and depression will be discussed in further detail shortly, in the section "Opening the Heart, Transforming the Mind."

The realization of our heart-mind has nothing to do with romantic sentimentalism, and it requires us to be naked of defenses. Then reality can penetrate our heart and our heart can penetrate reality. An old Buddhist saying states: "The whole universe is not big enough to contain our own heart, but our heart contains the whole universe."

Depression as a Loss of Heart

According to many doctors and psychologists, depression is one of the most widespread problems in the West in modern times.[7] Depression can be a symptom that arises when we lose contact with the depth of our heart. This "loss of heart" is a heavy feeling that contains repressed anger and resentment which stagnate in our bodies and turn into bitterness.

Confused by our ego-delusions, we freeze our feelings by imposing fabricated stories and judgments: "There is something wrong with me," "I'm inferior to others," "I must protect myself against others," or

"Those others are mean and are trying to hurt me." These subconscious judgments make depression a problem—not the vulnerable feelings of uncertainty, grief, anger, despair, or fear hidden underneath them. If you are suffering from depression, it is very important to see through these negative storylines and reconnect with your true heart. As we cautioned in the Introduction, those with acute depression should seek proper medical and psychological assistance.

Not only does a loss of heart give rise to depression, it also leads to more dangerous illnesses. In his book *Core Energetics,* Dr. John Pierrakos writes about evaluating ten patients with cardiovascular disease at Montefiore Hospital. What he discovered was that the common denominator among these ten patients was their inability to accept feelings. He also discovered this same inability among his own cardiovascular patients.

OPENING THE HEART, TRANSFORMING THE MIND

What shuts down our heart quicker than anything else? It's not letting ourselves have our own experience. It is judging, criticizing, and trying to make our experience something other than what it is. If we feel angry, needy, dependent, lonely, confused, sad, or scared, we imagine there's something wrong with us and place conditions on ourselves: "I should never feel like this again."

The stories we then make up are the ego's deluded way of freezing and controlling our experience. To feel our emotions directly and allow their energy to flow freely would threaten the ego. When we open to the actual sensation of a feeling, the ego, or "I"-notion, holding everything together dissolves into "is-ness," which is the larger reality of who we are.

The pain of feeling the hurt beneath our feelings is the pain of the ego being challenged. When this pain pierces the ego's protective shell, the ego wants to fight back. We make up stories about these feelings to perpetuate the ego and maintain the status quo. We hinder the transformation of emotions by creating stories about them. On the other hand, the pain of letting go of the stories and feeling the hurt beneath these feelings opens our heart. It allows anger to transform into communication, fear to transform into clarity, jealousy into empathy, and so on—and thus nurtures compassion for ourselves and others.

We take a big step when we open our hearts to the accumulated feelings stagnating in our body-mind.[8] This begins the process of going beyond numbness to become aware and alive again. This is the practice of waking up!

In the following chapters you will be reminded to always maintain awareness of your heart-mind connection. This awareness of your heart is the basis of following the Great Heart Way successfully. One way of being aware of our heart in the broadest spiritual sense is to practice being mindful of the physical heart when working with negative thoughts and emotions. This fact of being aware of your physical heart is what we call the heart-mind connection. Just allow all the thoughts and raw emotions created over limitless time to manifest. Without holding onto or identifying with them, just feel them and let them be. Staying with them isn't easy or comfortable. It can be challenging, frightening, even excruciating, especially in the beginning. But the more we do it, the easier it becomes and there is nothing more rewarding.

When we feel angry, jealous, envious, and full of judgments, we can use our heart awareness to acknowledge these feelings without interpreting, judging, or repressing them. By accepting ourselves as we are, our heart begins to open. This is the source of unconditional love, for ourselves *and* others, who are also seen and accepted as they are without being judged or ignored.

We can accept and feel our feelings—even when they are hateful—without judging ourselves for having them. This begins a process of transformation that stops us from harming ourselves or others. An old Chinese saying tells us that we are responsible for our actions, but not for our feelings. Feeling a feeling is not the same as acting it out: to feel like hurting someone is not the same as actually

hurting them. However, if we do not use our nonjudgmental awareness to recognize the origin of the feeling of wanting to hurt someone, there is a danger that we will feed the fire of wanting to hurt
someone by holding onto our stories and thoughts about doing it.
This is attaching to our feelings. The Indian sage Ramakrishna[9] when
referring to emotions said: "smoke still arises, but in the enlightened it
doesn't stick to the walls." It's not the emotion but the attachment to
the emotion that brings everyone suffering and pain. When the fire
gets out of control, we might actually turn the feelings into hurtful actions. Most of us have been conditioned to respond to anger with a
"knee jerk reaction." At the very first instant when our ego feels hurt,
it responds immediately with anger that can turn into hatred. And
then we might attack someone, verbally or physically. This is a destructive way to respond to life situations that buries us deeper into our
negative karma. When the desire to hurt others exists merely as a feeling, it's not a problem as long as we do not attach to it. It's just a bodily sensation passing through us.

We develop many strategies to avoid feeling our feelings. Eating excessively, sleeping excessively, or turning to sex and drugs or abusive
behaviors—these are just some of the ways we use negative energies
to experience pleasure and avoid pain. But avoiding feelings actually
creates much more pain than the original feelings themselves.

THE "NICE GUY"

*I had been in therapy and meditated regularly during the past
six years and had definitely seen improvement in my overall
mindset. However, certain obstacles and blind spots continued
to manifest in my day-to-day life. For example, I still ap-
proached the world suspiciously and from a distance. There*

was always a low level of irritation present in most of my rela-tionships and my outlook on life was primarily based on fear.

My life had not been an easy one. Growing up gay had ex-posed me to a lot of bigotry and violence. I adopted the persona of "nice guy" in order to placate any possible aggression to-wards me. I sought escape in fantasy and drug addiction and, for the next 15 years continued to lead a double life of a pleas-ant guy in public and a dark, depressed, and secretive guy in pri-vate. By the age of 30 I began psychotherapy and started a regular meditation practice, which, though extremely helpful still seemed to miss something deeper that lay hidden inside me.

One of my first realizations while at the Great Heart retreat was that I had internalized a particular belief about being gay, "I was not allowed to have anger. I was to be subservient and obsequious to those around me. Gay meant not quite a man." I had been called "sissy" and "faggot" and "wimp." These la-bels did not allow for rage. I accepted them and had, there-fore, been stuffing my anger for most of my life. I simply did not show anger.

Sitting on retreat I began to feel the old irritation and anxi-ety return. This time, however, I was encouraged to drop the story around it and just allow it to be there. The main thing was to stay in my body without judgment. While staying connected to my heart, what was a slight irritation quickly became anger and then a deep, profound feeling of rage swept over me. This was something I had been avoiding all my life. The freedom that I experienced in allowing my body to become consumed with this emotion was astounding. As I continued to connect with my heart, the rage transformed into grief. This grief brought to my awareness an image of myself at age 14. It was Halloween and I was dressed up, appropriately enough, as a fairy (with lipstick and all). When the other trick-or-treaters started to ridicule me, all of the shame and loneliness that I had experienced at that time came back to me and I realized that I had no one to protect me or tell me that I was special or validate my "gayness" at all. While sitting on the meditation cushion I began to weep. Focusing on this image, I offered myself all of the protection and care that I did not receive at the time. I could feel my heart beginning to open up.

This was only the beginning. As I continue to practice the Great Heart Way I realized that my body has much to teach me. There are secrets hidden inside me, and by staying present with my emotions, there is the real possibility of transformation. I am so grateful for this profound practice. It has offered me an antidote to spiritual avoidance and helped me to delve deeper into myself.

A hidden feeling is like a festering boil: it needs to be lanced in order to heal. If we're willing to go into a painful feeling, the healing process begins automatically. Feelings are not fixed energies. They naturally and constantly transmute from one feeling into another. By avoiding feelings, we stop that process of transmutation and the energy stagnates within us. Denied feelings—no matter what they are—are easier to bear than the *fear* of feeling them. So fear, itself, is more bearable than the fear of the fear. It's the same with anger, frustration, and so on.

Jesus said, "If you bring forth what is in you, what you bring forth will save you. If you do not bring forth what is within you, what you do not bring forth will kill you."[10] The irony is that the defenses we create to protect us from pain create more pain. In the process, we deny important aspects of ourselves. They need to be reintegrated if we want to be whole, healthy, spontaneous beings, capable of helping ourselves and others.

The only way to undo the negative karma we've created is by peacefully connecting with our heart and abiding in that awareness, without impatience and without expectations.

By deconstructing our defenses, fixed images, and hidden assumptions, we discover the original nature of our mind, which is clear, bright, and skillful. And when we stop living from habit and open up our heart-mind, we will be able to manifest peace, love, and compassion.

EMOTIONS AS KARMA

According to Hindu and Buddhist laws of karma, everything we do has an effect.[11] The word "karma" has come into the popular culture, but not everybody actually understands what it means. Karma is the universal law of cause and effect. All potentialities exist in our lives, but due to our "deeds" (the precise translation of "karma") only certain potentialities come to fruition. Deeds include our thoughts, speech, and actions. They plant the seeds of different possible results, or effects, which may grow or not, according to the conditions. Some seeds sprout immediately. Others take decades to sprout or even appear in other lifetimes. But according to the laws of karma, they will eventually have an effect.

We have seen how our shadow is composed of all those aspects of ourselves that we've condemned, rejected, and ignored, and which subsequently retreat to our unconscious mind. Carl Jung wrote that the shadow is made up of the personality's tendencies, motives, and traits that a person considers shameful for one reason or another and seeks to repress.[12] When they're repressed, they become unconscious and are projected onto others. The more parts of ourselves we condemn, the bigger the unconscious bag we carry and the greater its projection onto the world. Projections cloud our view of reality.

When our behavior is controlled by unconscious influences, the results are invariably negative. Similarly, when we reject aspects of ourselves, we create negative karma that constrains our lives. When conditions are right, the negative karma we carry in our shadow manifests as various problems and conflicts in our life. Our shadow is a storehouse of that karma.

In the Bible we find the concept of karma, though obviously not by that name: In Galatians 6:7 it says, "For whatsoever a man sows, that shall he also reap." In Hosea 8:7 it says, "For they have sown the wind and they shall reap the whirlwind." In Luke 6:38 it says, "The measure you give will be the measure you get back." And in Proverbs 22:16 it says "He who oppresses the poor to increase his own wealth and he who gives to the rich shall surely come to want." These are simple, straightforward statements of how karma works in our lives. The modern version is "What goes around comes around."

One of our students, a young doctor named Antonia, discovered a more sophisticated example of how her family's karma was passed from generation to generation.

ANTONIA'S FAMILY KARMA

As I was sitting in meditation with the pain of a recently ended relationship, I noticed that the ending of relationships always threw me for a loop. Of course, isn't that true for everyone? As the song goes, "breaking up is hard to do." But for me, there was something deeper: a feeling of failure and a complete loss of perspective. When I sat with this in meditation, I realized there was also a sense of old childhood feelings at play—and a sense that the karma entangled with my sense of failure and loss was greater than me, that it went deep into my family's history.

As I meditated with these feelings, my mother kept coming to mind. I did not understand what my mother had to do with this break-up; it didn't make sense to me. But I stayed with the feelings and tried not to judge them.

Soon an image came to me of my mother's grandmother, my great-grandmother. It was a picture of her I had seen many times, the only picture my family had of her. She wore a long dress and glasses. She was smiling, but the smile seemed forced and her eyes were very sad. Not long after this photograph was taken, my great-grandmother committed suicide.

The memory of my mother's father also came up. After his mother (my great-grandmother) committed suicide, he began to drink heavily. Ultimately, he drank himself to death, dying of cirrhosis at a young age. My mother, who was only 35 when he died, had spent much of her young life trying to "save" her father from the pain of his own mother's death.

As I continued to sit with these feelings and images, without judging or elaborating on them, I realized my mother had made an assumption: "I failed to save my father." And she carried that sadness from the time that he died. I also saw how she plays out this belief in her relationships. Determined to "be there" for others, she is never there for herself. It's as if she does not deserve happiness, because she could not save her father.

Then my own father came to mind. He was mistreated by his mother, who was in no way loving or supportive. As a result, my father spent a lifetime abusing drugs, alcohol, and food. This resulted in many health problems. Recently I gave up hope of "saving him" and accepted that, due to his myriad health problems, he would probably soon die.

Compounding this issue was the old wound of my parent's divorce, which took place when I was four years old. Not only had my mother failed to save her father, who died the year before, she had failed to save my father, who then left her.

As I sat with these images and feelings, I realized I had done the same thing as my mother. I had invested a lot of energy into trying to "save" my father. Because I wasn't able to do so, I had a sense of failure. As a result, I developed my mother's strategy in relationships: I give up all my needs and desires, trying to be the "perfect woman" for my partner.

My mother and I both dealt with the guilt of not being able to save our fathers by trying to be perfect women for our romantic partners. By being the person our partners most wanted us to be, maybe we could heal the damage our grandmothers had done and make up for the pain of not being able to save our fathers.

When my relationships ended, my pattern was to spiral into a sense of overwhelming failure and inadequacy. On top of the natural pain of a relationship ending, I piled on the family karma of "a woman failing a man." Suddenly I could see this pattern clearly: my great-grandmother had "failed" my grandfather, my mother had "failed" my grandfather, my grandmother had "failed" my father, my mother and I had both "failed" my father.

In romantic relationships with men, I was there as "the rescuer"—even when no one needed rescuing. The way I rescued men was by trying to be the woman I thought they wanted me to be, rather than being myself. This is what I had always done with my father; and I had learned it from my mother, who had done it with every man I'd ever seen her with.

Suddenly I felt an incredible rush of energy as I freed up the feelings of guilt and failure that accompanied the grief of my ended relationship. I realized these other feelings were extra, that I need only feel the grief. And then something shifted. The awful pain I had been feeling became more bearable: sadness, poignancy, but nothing unmanageable. The sense of complete "overwhelm" was gone.

This experience taught me that in future relationships, I can simply be myself. Intellectually, I have known this for a long time, but now I feel it in my body. I also realize that I can't really "fail" in a relationship. Relationships come and go; they're not about success or failure. Really, for me it's about being myself and knowing that I no longer have to carry forth the burden of this family karma. It's hard to express in words what a relief this is.

DENIED FEELINGS AS NEGATIVE KARMA

Many people blame the world, circumstances, friends, life partners, or parents for life's misfortunes. As our spiritual practice matures, however, we realize that whatever happens to us is a product of our own karma. Naturally we may ask, "What is this karma?" Usually we think of the effects of karma, of our actions, as happening sometime in the future. We aren't clear about how we create karma and how this karma is with us in the present moment.

Karma is compounded by all those aspects of our mind that have not been acknowledged. Negative karma is a consequence of denied feelings that then manifest in devious attitudes. In error, we think that what we ignore and repress doesn't exist. We cannot just hide our heads in the ground like ostriches; even if we ignore or repress them, our inner issues are at work.

One of our students, Martin, had repressed feelings of anger since childhood. As an adult, Martin had no memory of condemning his anger and putting it into his shadow-bag. As a child, however, he grew up in a dysfunctional family with alcoholic parents who yelled at him and beat him whenever he expressed his anger. To survive in that environment, Martin learned to repress his anger. Unconsciously he also repressed feelings of joy and love.

Feelings express the life of the body. Feelings are the body's natural response to specific situations. They result from the perception of some inner movement. If there is no movement, there is no life. In his book *Joy,* Alexander Lowen adds, "Suppressing one feeling suppresses all feelings. If we suppress our fear, we suppress our anger. Suppressing anger results in the suppression of love."[13]

For Martin, numbing his feelings as a child was the best he could do to cope with his situation. The consequences of this are now affecting his adult life. Martin carries with him an inner anguish that intensifies when he becomes close to others. As a result, he isolates himself and feels there is an insurmountable wall between him and the world.

As his awareness increased, Martin started to feel his inner pain. By expanding his awareness in meditation, he began to identify his feelings and to get in touch with his repressed anger. Old memories opened up to his conscious mind. Realizing that the inner pain originated with his denial of childhood feelings, his numbness started to dissolve. As Martin continued the steps of the Great Heart Way, he was able to start new relationships.

Like Martin, many of us condemn feelings that are not socially "acceptable." We try desperately to fit in and be approved by parents, peers, and institutions. Parents often tell children that they're "bad" for having certain feelings, such as anger or sexual feelings. And it's common for families to admonish children when they are frightened, saying things like "You shouldn't feel like that," "Toughen up," "Boys don't cry," or "Don't be a wimp." These attitudes cause children to suppress their true feelings and superimpose a fake attitude.

Suppressing their fear doesn't make children brave; it only puts them in conflict. If the fear (or anger, in Martin's case) is too great, the child may unconsciously suppress *all feelings* at once. By repressing one feeling, all other feelings become repressed—because we are suppressing the overall sensitivity and vitality of the body. When feelings are quashed over a long period of time, chronic depression sets in. Martin was living in the chronic state of pain known as "depression."

We learn early on that certain feelings are "bad" and others are "good." All societies and religions have moral codes of behavior. One version of the Ten Commandments states: "You shall not covet your neighbor's wife." It is a sin to desire a married woman; but if she is attractive, it would be natural for someone to feel attracted to her. To have this feeling is not the sin; the sin is attaching to the feeling and *acting* on it.

In the interest of social harmony, we follow certain rules of behavior. These rules do not prevent an individual from having feelings. We have no control over what feelings arise and when they arise. When we repress our feelings, we block the flow of our energy, our creative life force, and our vitality.

Society labels certain feelings, such as fear and anger, as "negative feelings." But feelings, in and of themselves, are neither negative nor positive. To condemn feelings as good or bad is to condemn the person—ourselves or others—rather than the actions. The way we discharge our feelings may result in negative *actions,* but we never have to justify how we feel. So-called negative feelings are not antagonistic to life; when they are accepted, they are very valuable aspects of a person.

Anger, for example, can be a natural response to oppression. There is a widespread confusion between anger and hatred. Hatred is an expression of anger with the intent to hurt; it's like a knife that's intended to inflict a wound. Anger, on the other hand, can be an energetic reaction of unease that erupts spontaneously in certain circumstances.

When anger arises, connect with your heart and spend a few minutes looking at the anger. Be aware of your breathing. When we feel anger there is always an emotional hurt underneath it. Connect with that hurt. Ask yourself, "What am I hurt about?" Do you feel that someone transgressed against you? In what way? When you find what the hurt is about, you must feel the pain directly without blaming anyone. Keep connecting with your heart and let go of the story lines and directly feel the unpleasant physical sensations or physical pain associated with the emotional hurt. This way your heart will open up and you can approach the situation from a much wider perspective. Practicing meditation and cultivating heart-mind awareness gives us the opportunity to respond to our emotions in a nonviolent, compassionate way.

Denied feelings, on the other hand, are like waves on the sea: they multiply. When we feel sad, it doesn't stop there; we start feeling sad about feeling sad. Then we feel sad about feeling sad about feeling sad. There is no end to it—and no hope of change as long as we reject our negative feelings. In *Bioenergetics* Alexander Lowen, M.D., says,

> *The life of an individual is the life of his body....A person who doesn't breathe deeply reduces the life of his body...If he doesn't feel fully he narrows the life of his body...In effect, most people go through life on a limited budget of energy and feeling.*[14]

When feelings are denied, the ways they reappear can be devious and twisted. Depression, hatred, revenge, and false kindness are examples of the karmic consequences of denied feelings; and these distorted attitudes generate more negative karma. The effects of denied feelings can emerge in more subtle ways, such as a cynical attitude toward life, playful teasing that has malicious undertones, passive-aggressive behavior, and holding grudges against others.

The way to get out of this destructive cycle and find inner happiness is to bring our denied feelings into the conscious awareness of our heart-mind. Until we begin to actually feel our emotions, we will keep looking for happiness outside ourselves and, sadly, we will never find it.

Recognizing that she had repressed her feelings, a student named Dahlia told us:

> *The assumption that my feelings aren't important colored much of my life. Rather than expressing my anger and hate, it just oozed out in subtle ways over long periods of time. I'd hold slight grudges, tease people inappropriately, or do little things to annoy or get back at them—taking twisted pleasure in these expressions of negativity. Now, I have given myself permission to feel anger when it arises and hatred when it arises. They usually dissolve on their*

*own in a very short time. Then I don't have to lug them around
with me or hurt others.*

Many of us turn away from emotions because we don't know how
to work with them. Emotions are not to be taken as thoughts. When
negative thoughts arise, we can just let them be, without judging or
identifying with them. Emotions must be handled differently.

When strong emotions arise in our body and mind, we must connect with our heart and feel the emotions thoroughly. We do this
without interpreting the emotions and without identifying with their
storylines: "I shouldn't feel that way because..." or "There must be
something wrong with me if I feel this way because..." As long as our
feelings are flowing we can work with them. *Interpreting* them with
stories, making them "mean something," freezes them. Then our emotions become rock hard and block our life force.

Some people might think that they are feeling their emotions
when they are actually avoiding them. They are only interpreting a
feeling before they feel it. For example, at the first sign of anxiety,
many people will take a pill, go shopping, take a nap, or get in a fight
with someone. Reacting to emotions in this way is not feeling one's
emotions, but is avoiding or suppressing them. Actually feeling emotions is quite different. In order to feel anxiety you have to experience
the sensation of the feeling without trying to change it. Stay completely immersed within the awareness of the anxious sensations.
Connect with your heart. Breathe deeply and take a few minutes to
fully experience the bodily sensations of the anxiety. By feeling the
anxiety, you will notice the feeling of fear that is covered over by the
anxiety. Then move your attention to the fear and feel it thoroughly.
When you feel the fear and let go of your stories about the fear, you
will discover some emotional pain. Maintain your mental connection
to your heart throughout this process. As you connect with this pain
underlying your feelings, the pain will start to shift.

Darla, a young mother, had been having trouble letting go of her persistent anxiety and depression. Here she describes how connecting with her heart broke her log jam of feelings and emotions.

▬▬▬▬▬ DARLA'S FARM HOUSE ▬▬▬▬▬

I focused my attention on connecting with my heart and feeling thoroughly the anxious sensations throughout my body. At 3 A.M. when the baby woke up to have his bottle, I continued connecting with my heart and feeling the fear underneath the anxiety while I fed him.

I remembered then the time when my parents had told me they were getting divorced. I had started crying very hard, but was ashamed of crying. This shameful feeling seemed strange to me, because what would be more natural for a child than to cry at such painful news? Why was I ashamed? I did not try to answer that question. I just felt the pain underneath my feelings of shame and kept my heart-mind connection. Then another lost memory came to my mind. I remembered the farm house where we had lived before my parents had separated, my room and the trees in the yard. I felt a great sadness and cried for a long time, missing my home and realizing that ever since, I have never felt at home. Then the phrase "I am not safe" sprung into my head, and I realized this is how I have felt since my parents' separation. Suddenly, I saw that many of my fears and constant anxiety stem from this feeling of insecurity. Maintaining the heart-mind connection helped to open this up for me and gave me a sense of strength and acceptance of my feelings no matter how painful.

Going into our feelings like this, rather than going away from them like we usually do, is a safe way to heal our old hurts so we do not have to continue to carry them around. Until we learn to feel our emotions we are like Prince Hal in Shakespeare's play *King Henry IV, Part 1* who "doth permit the base contagious clouds to smother up his beauty from the world." Ignored emotional pain is like a dark cloud that obscures the sun.

The Great Heart Way is not an invitation to drop thinking and just feel. It is an invitation to learn to think when it is time to think and to feel when it is time to feel. The Great Heart Way is an invitation to harmonize body and mind so they work as a unified reality rather than a chaotic dysfunction.

EPHEMERAL HAPPINESS, EMOTIONAL PAIN

Everybody wants to be happy. We go down all kinds of avenues to find happiness only to discover that most of them are dead ends. The Western ideal is to find happiness through wealth, fame, good looks, and an attractive partner. Unfortunately, good looks fade; and judging by the number of unhappy celebrities, wealth and fame do not guarantee happiness. We all have the potential for happiness, but we get distracted by attachments and desires that subvert this potential.

There is a story about how hunters trap monkeys in India. They take a coconut and cut a hole in it large enough for the monkey to insert his hand, but small enough so the hand can't be withdrawn when the monkey makes a fist. Then the hunter puts some bait—food or something shiny—in the coconut and ties it to a tree. When the monkey grabs the bait, he is trapped. All he has to do to free himself is release the bait. But this trap is very effective, because the monkey won't let go. In the same way, we human beings get trapped by our ideas of happiness—and we won't let them go, even at the risk of our lives.

Do our attachments bring us happiness? Material possessions might amuse us for a short time, but then we need something new to maintain the euphoria. And relationships—judging by the divorce rate—don't guarantee happiness either. We get tired of our spouse and look elsewhere for excitement. Then we get tired of the new relationship. We need someone else to feel alive. And we repeat this same pattern again and again.

There is nothing inherently bad about material possessions or relationships. When we learn to release attachments, we can thoroughly enjoy them without feeling avarice, jealousy, or guilt. But until then, they bring only momentarily pleasure and happiness. This happiness fades because it's based on attachment to impermanent things. Our attachments to emotional and psychological states—attitudes, beliefs, projections, images of the way things should be—bring us as much unhappiness as attachment to material things.

A traditional Zen story tells of two monks on a pilgrimage.[15] One day they encounter a woman on the banks of a swollen river. One of the monks offers to carry her across the river, and she accepts. Then the monks continue their pilgrimage. The second monk is unusually quiet for the rest of the day. Finally, as they settle down to sleep that night, he says, "We took vows as monks not to touch women. But back at the river you actually *carried* a woman. If I had known you were that kind of monk, I wouldn't have gone on this pilgrimage with you." To which the first monk replied, "Are you still carrying that woman? I put her down on the river bank."

With so many attachments to our ideas of right and wrong, we're unable to be flexible or to respond spontaneously and appropriately to situations as they arise. It's no wonder we can't find happiness.

Chronic Pain and Healing Pain

Basically there are two kinds of emotional pain and two kinds of happiness. *Chronic emotional pain* is a symptom of our denied feelings. We try to overcome this pain by looking outside of ourselves for happiness based on our material or mental desires. It gives rise to *ephemeral happiness,* which may last a day, a week, a month, a year. But when the buzz fades, we're left with the same chronic pain. On the other hand, there is *true happiness* and *healing pain.* Going through the healing pain of recovering our denied feelings is the source of real, true happiness. To find true happiness, we must bring peace to those parts of ourselves that are in unconscious torment.

Attachment to Pain

In one Great Heart workshop, several participants noted that in their Protestant upbringing it would be considered "self-indulgent" to allow oneself to feel inner pain, when there is so much "real" suffering in the world, so many people lacking proper nutrition and good health. We, on the other hand, are well fed and in reasonably good health. Why should we indulge in our own suffering?

Indulging in pain for the sake of pain is masochism. If we somehow gratuitously seek out feeling sad and depressed and then choose to remain that way, we are indulging in pain. What the Great Heart Way asks you to do is to genuinely feel the inner pain that is already present in you in order to heal that stagnant energy. Feeling pain to *heal* pain is very different from indulging in pain.

An Indian sage once said that joy is everywhere, the whole world is a creation of joy.[16] If a human being's most natural state is one of happiness and joy, why don't we meet many truly happy people these days?

You may be incredulous to hear that we prefer to remain in familiar states of pain, rather than open up to a deeper and happier life. If realizing joy requires us to probe the dark, unknown aspects of our personality, we may choose to remain in chronic pain. We may try to ignore our inner pain for long periods of time. But, unfortunately, this just causes us to live in a constant state of insecurity and anxiety, because we are haunted by our worst fears about ourselves as we continue to repress our emotions. Denied pain can erupt in emotional illness or even serious physical breakdowns.

In his book *Quantum Healing,* Deepak Chopra writes:

> *In the 1970s a series of important discoveries began, centering on a new class of minute chemicals called neurotransmitters. As their name implies, these chemicals transmit nerve impulses; they act in our bodies as "communicator molecules," whereby the neurons of the brain can talk to the rest of the body.*

Neurotransmitters are the runners that race to and from the brain, telling every organ inside us of our emotions, desires, memories, intuitions, and dreams. None of these events are confined to the brain alone. Likewise, none of them are strictly mental, since they can be coded into chemical messages. Neurotransmitters touch the life of every cell.

Thoughts and emotions create a physical response in the body. Thinking and feeling involves brain chemistry, which promotes a cascade of other bodily responses. This reality may encourage us to be more aware of how we identify with and react to our thoughts and feelings.

We have control over how we react. The thought of hurting someone, for example, could lead to negative results or it could dissipate on its own. A feeling of jealousy could cause us to act compulsively or could be used for spiritual growth. With the practice of meditation and the development of awareness, we learn to observe our thoughts and we learn how to avoid being swept away by them. When the thought of hurting someone comes to our mind, we say "Aha! Look at that!" We can immediately make an inventory of our body. Am I feeling hurt? We can learn to connect with our heart and to feel the pain until it passes away. Emotions and thoughts arise and pass away. If we learn to be one with this process, without claiming ownership of our thoughts and emotions, we won't create stagnant energy in our body. Canadian physician Gabor Maté has written extensively on this:

> There is a growing awareness in our culture—or despite our culture—that health and spirituality are linked. Health, in other words, rests on four pillars, all necessary to support the complete edifice that is the human being: body; mind, including conscious thought and conscious and unconscious emotions; the soul; and our social connections with other people. We suffer, physically and emotionally, when we neglect any of these four pillars of health. Emotional repression is, in our society, a major contributor to all significant illnesses.
>
> People who develop cancer or multiple sclerosis or ALS or any of the autoimmune diseases, such a rheumatoid arthritis, or conditions like chronic fatigue syndrome, fibromyalgia, endometriosis or migraine headaches—to name only a few—all share lifelong emotional patterns of self-suppression...I have seen such patterns repeatedly in my two dozen years of family practice and also in many years of palliative-care work.[17]

As a primary step in preventative medicine, we as a culture should consider teaching people of all ages, including seniors and children, how to meditate. They could then get in touch with their deepest being; and they could create a safe inner space where thoughts and emotions dissolve on their own, without causing harm to the body. However, there are many diseases that have a physiological origin and should be treated by qualified physicians. We do not recommend that you try to heal your physical ailments on your own, but many of our complaints can be traced to emotional roots as well.

Dr. Daniel Goleman confirms this observation in his book *Emotional Intelligence:*

> The cumulative evidence for adverse medical effects from anger, anxiety and depression is compelling. Both anger and anxiety, when chronic, can make people more susceptible to a range of diseases…. Helping people better manage their upsetting feelings— anger, anxiety, depression, pessimism and loneliness—is a form of disease prevention. Since the data show that the toxicity of these emotions, when chronic, is on a par with smoking cigarettes, helping people handle them better could potentially have a medical payoff as great as getting heavy smokers to quit.

Real Happiness, Healing Pain

True satisfaction lies within us. To reveal it, we must first enter into our chronic pain and recover the tormented feelings buried beneath it. These buried feelings belong to the child that we were. As children we were spontaneously innocent and free, but we've lost touch with that innocence and freedom. To rescue this, we must embark on the inner journey.

Psychiatrist Alexander Lowen writes that an emotionally healthy person can display a large range of emotions in a short amount of time.[18] Jealousy can turn into grief, which can turn into loving feelings. In Colorado, we say if you don't like the weather just wait a few minutes and it will change. These changes are like waves on the surface of the ocean. They don't disturb the deep calm that gives us a sense of joy and fulfillment.

When we inhibit the flow of feelings by weaving stories about them, their energy stagnates. In the practice of meditation, however, its raw aliveness is accessed directly in a nonconceptual way. We open to the bodily sensations of feelings without trying to discover their "meaning." As we mentioned before, when feelings of fear, anxiety, anger, or jealousy arise (or whatever the feeling might be), connect with your heart and make a conscious effort to approach the feeling directly without having any preconceptions about it or weaving stories to interpret it. The actual meaning of a feeling can only be clear to us after we have felt it completely. In this way the energy is transformed: anger, for example, can transform into sadness, which can transform into joy. By just being with the energy of feelings, without interpretation, we learn the language of the body and tap into the body's ancient wisdom. Beyond shallow ego-centered feelings, we discover a larger expanse of true happiness, well-being, and unconditional love.

Nobody can deny there is pain in life. But the pain of being truly alive is very different than the pain of being dead to our true feelings. Every child is born with a joyful heart, but pressures and demands of family, society, and life often break our spirit. And then, joy is lost. To retrieve our birthright of joy and true happiness, we must journey into the realms of the unconscious.

SPIRITUAL BYPASSING AND KARMA

Some spiritual leaders try to bypass the importance of the unconscious mind, when trying to effect permanent change in their followers' behavioral patterns. They may say, "Think good thoughts. Have good feelings." But adding good feelings on top of our shadow-bag of repressed feelings is like adding frosting to a rotten cake. It's like going to the dentist with a toothache and having the dentist cover the decay with a beautiful white filling without first taking care of the cavity. What happens then? We only increase the pain. The same happens when we superimpose good thoughts and feelings on our shadow-bag.

To really effect change in our life, we must try to address the root of the problem and not suppress the symptoms. Used properly, symptoms are the gateway to true healing and peace.

The experience of a spiritual insight can momentarily transcend our shadow, or negative karma. I (Shinko) experienced such moments of transcendence during Zen meditation retreats. I realized that the Universe and my mind are the same, and that all sentient beings are none other than my self. Having these experiences brought me a great deal of joy. Nevertheless, when I returned home from these retreats, all the joy would suddenly disappear, and my old pattern of unhappiness would take over again.

A disconnection between equanimity in meditation and dishar-mony in our life is very common, even for experienced meditators. It was recognized in the thirteenth century by Japanese Zen Master Do-gen, who wrote: "Entering the deep mountains and thinking about the enlightened way is comparatively easy, while building temples and making religious statues it is very difficult."[19] In modern terms, "building temples and making statues" represents working in the world and raising a family. Zen or any spiritual practice does not end when a meditator has experienced deep spiritual insight. That insight or wisdom needs to manifest in one's life. This step requires us to look deeply at all of the resistance we have to being present when uncom-fortable feelings or situations arise in our life. Then the cycle contin-ues—since when wisdom deepens, how we integrate it in our life also deepens. Unless we can be comfortable with all aspects of ourselves, including our emotional body, we will never be able to realize this in-tegral life.

As long as I (Shinko) could remember, I always thought it was somehow "safer" to be unhappy than to be happy. I never questioned this belief, I just blindly followed it—which made me unconsciously choose situations that would not bring me happiness.

When I was younger, I entered into a relationship with a man who suffered from chronic depression. We had very little in common except this attachment to unhappiness. I lived in inner contradiction. My heart yearned for happiness and fulfillment, but my fear of happiness kept me trapped in an unhappy, unfulfilling life. Because I could see this contradiction between my feelings and my actions, I started to meditate. Through the practice of meditation, I developed awareness of my mind and my life. Eventually I was able to move on from that relationship.

Each one of us creates our own life. Our individual karma tints our different experiences of reality. Some of us are optimists, and others are pessimists. What determines our outlook? In order to understand our own karma, we need to cultivate awareness. Through meditation and heart-mind awareness, I could feel clearly that guilt underlay my fear of happiness—but guilt from what? Where did it come from? In chapter 5, I will disclose what I discovered.

Awareness or mindfulness is the ability to connect with our hearts and to observe thoughts, feelings, and reactions without judgment. This ability opens us up to the world, to the universe, to every single sentient being—and to a deep compassion beyond ego—so we can illuminate our individual negative karma and transform it.

EXERCISES

Sit in meditation for at least twenty minutes daily. If you have to skip a day, that's okay, but return to your daily schedule of meditation as soon as you can. When you finish your meditation, spend some time answering the questions below. You don't have to remain in meditation posture; you can sit at a table to write your answers. Depending on your time, do one or more. Record your answers in your journal.

These questions will help you identify your hidden beliefs. If any of them bring up a strong emotional response, connect with your heart and take time to feel the physical sensation of that emotion.

Breathe deeply. Let go of the storyline and return your focus to the physical sensation. And continue to breathe deeply. Your responses to the exercises are neither good nor bad. They just are. For now, remember to maintain a nonjudgmental attitude when you answer the questions. This means to accept the answers without judging whether they are right or wrong, taking them with the same accepting attitude that compassionate parents have for their infant. They accept the infant whether she or he is calm or crying. In the same way, we recommend that you accept your answers—whatever they are—without judging them.

Meditation is the foundation of the Great Heart Way. Following the instructions in this book on how to meditate, and doing so regularly, are the keys to effectively put this method into practice. Learning how to focus the mind is of great importance, because when we learn to meditate we begin to experience some detachment from our thoughts and feelings. This detachment helps us to work with the following exercise to effectively bring the Great Heart Way into our lives. It signals that we are starting to experience that we are actually more than our thoughts and feelings and that we are a large container in which thoughts and feelings can arise and dissolve.

As we mentioned in the introduction, we recommend that you read this book (while you are developing your meditation practice) at least once before you attempt to do the exercises. There is a lot of information throughout the book that will teach you how to work with the feelings and thoughts that may arise when doing these exercises. The exercises may create strong feelings in you, but these feelings are great opportunities to practice the Great Heart Way.

To provide a bit of summary instruction:

If uncomfortable feelings arise, do not try to overpower them. Just breathe. Connect with your heart and feel the pain underlying the discomfort. Let go of the storyline about the feelings. Then ask yourself, "Where does the pain come from?" In this way, the answer will be sprouting from the actual pain that is emanating from somewhere in your body. It won't be just an abstraction or fictitious story that you create in your head in order to avoid feeling the sensation in depth. It is very different when the answer springs into your consciousness from your body than from your head. You will feel the answer with your whole body as a release of energy. Then set that answer aside and keep feeling whatever sensations arise. The same procedure will apply if any of the following questions make you feel very angry. Take a deep breath. Connect with your heart and allow yourself to feel the anger. Where is it in your body? Do not try to justify the anger, but instead feel the pain underlying it. What is this pain about? Let go of any answers that appear and just keep feeling. If you can follow these steps you are already practicing the Great Heart Way. Always record your answers in your journal.

You do not need to work with these exercises within any particular time frame. You can take as much or as little time as you want. We recommend you approach the exercises after you have practiced meditation, because your mind will be more open and spontaneous. At that time you can decide how many questions you want to answer.

If nothing comes to mind regarding a particular question, that's okay. Just skip it for now. You can always try again later. Something might arise for you when you least expect it.

During meditation you should focus your mind on your breathing, not these exercises. But if when working with them you feel the need to sit in meditation again to think quietly about an exercise or to connect with your heart and feel your emotions, we encourage you to do that.

1. Situations that reoccur in our lives may seem random or co-incidental. Looking more deeply, we may find these events occur as the result of hidden images and beliefs formed early in life. To transform these, we must first become aware of them. Settling the mind in meditation makes it possible to

concentrate on these subtle issues. After sitting in meditation, write your answers to the following questions:

- a. Are there reoccurring patterns of feelings or situations in your life that appear to be random and unconnected to anything in particular?
- b. What situations make you angry?
- c. What situations make you sad?
- d. Do you feel like a victim of circumstances? When?
- e. What kind of people do you hate?
- f. What kind of people do you love?
- g. Do you get in trouble at work or school? What happens when you do?
- h. How do you feel when you meet new people?

These questions will give you clues to what is relevant or important for you.

2. Reflecting on these seemingly random patterns or situations, what emotions do you associate with them? Write down how you feel when these incidents occur.

Connect with your heart and just feel. Do not identify with any thoughts that might arise about these feelings. Do not listen to any stories fabricated in your head about them. If there are stories in your mind, don't fight them. Just return your attention to the sensations and feel them with your whole body. Record your experiences in your journal.

4

THE EGO'S FIXED IMAGES OF SELF

If you hate a person, you hate something in that person that is part of yourself. What isn't part of ourselves doesn't disturb us.

—HERMANN HESSE[1]

In the gaps between thoughts, non-conceptual wisdom shines continually.

—MILAREPA[2]

EGO IDENTITY AND THE SPLIT FROM OUR ORIGINAL MIND

When we are born, our awareness is open and receptive. As infants, our egos are not yet developed and we do not differentiate between self and "not self." Our first experience of duality seemed to be on the physical level. Some things like hunger or wetness are unpleasant and cause us dissatisfaction and pain. Others, like feeding or a gentle touch, are pleasurable and bring a sense of satisfaction. Instinctively we seek to maximize experiences that produce pleasure and minimize those that produce pain. Thus these first impressions of life begin to condition our existence.[3]

Duality is soon experienced on the emotional level as well. As toddlers, we discover that certain feelings and behaviors produce negative or unpleasant consequences—primarily in the form of our parents' reactions. Based on the reactions they arouse, these early experiences begin to define for us "good feelings and behaviors" versus "bad feelings and behaviors." Dualities proliferate as we attempt to enhance those reactions from parents that feel good and to avoid or reduce those that feel bad. We try to limit our experience to the small territory of positive bodily sensations, happy feelings, and nice thoughts—while all the rest is perceived as "other," different from "self."

Thus, at an early age our original undivided mind is conditioned to think in terms of self/other, good/bad, love/hate, and so on. This fundamental sense of split further develops our ego identity.

As young children we depend on our parents and others to help us see and know ourselves. Inevitably, we internalize their responses. Based on their perceptions of us, we soon establish a sense of a separate "self," or ego identity—which simply means taking ourselves to be *something,* based on how others perceive and relate to us.[4]

As children, we attach to our feelings. When we are shocked by an event, our feelings can be too overwhelming for our young nervous system to handle. And our mind is not developed enough to make sense of them. As a result, we learn to contract our body and shut off our mind like a circuit breaker, in order to prevent our nervous system from blowing up. As a way of protecting ourselves, we become numbed to the shocking events.

The impressions of these early events—and the conclusions we draw from them—retreat into our unconscious mind. Because our intellect is not fully developed, each impression conveys a narrow conception of reality. Nevertheless, this limited concept of reality becomes part of our early programming. Frozen in our unconscious mind, it becomes one of the ingredients of our self image—a fixed image that will condition and color all of our adult lives.

In this way, we become emotionally handicapped. We are unable to function in situations that evoke the very feelings that we've rejected. The rejection of our feelings creates a first layer of pain. By running away from the situations that evoke these rejected feelings, we create a second layer of pain. Depression is a symptom of the layers of inner pain we create by rejecting our true feelings—and ultimately our true self.

Our ego identity is a deeply ingrained construct. From childhood through puberty and adulthood, we construct idealized notions of who we should be. To support this fabrication, we end up identifying with our possessions, reputation, relationships, personal history, and achievements. But identifying with external things never brings us true and lasting satisfaction or security. Our ego-centered world is a superficial form of reality that only prevents us from experiencing the deeper and boundless reality of who we truly are.

PETER'S FIRST IMPRESSIONS

Like most of us, Peter's mind was conditioned by his early impressions of life. As many children do, Peter wanted exclusive love from his parents. He did not want to share his parent's love with anyone. He didn't like seeing his parents loving his siblings; and he didn't like seeing his parents loving each other. He wanted all their love for himself. This kind of exclusive love is, of course, not possible. But whenever Peter didn't get his way, he took it as proof that he wasn't loved at all. Feeling unloved, he then felt hatred and hostility toward his parents. And since he had been taught that only bad people hate, he believed that he wasn't a good person.

Because the shock of such painful feelings and beliefs is too much for a child to endure, Peter retreated into a world of numbness. His body and mind became numb, to the extent that he lost all memory of these events. They became the hidden karma that would condition his adult actions.

Peter's thoughts of hating his parents caused an impression in his mind that resulted in his consequent belief of not being good. When they are tied together, the impression and the belief harden into a fixed self-image. When we have thoughts of hatred as adults, we can deal with them in a positive and creative way without acting on them. But a five-year-old child does not know how to deal with his thoughts. Like the Third Zen Ancestor in China wrote, "Thoughts are just like flowers in the air. Why do we work so hard at grasping them?"[5] Peter felt guilty and shameful, and he said to himself, "I must be a terrible person to have such feelings. And if I'm really that terrible, the only way to make up for it is to try to be completely perfect and loving in every way." Seeing love and hate as two opposite forces obscured Peter's undivided Original Mind and created deluded attitudes in his life.

As children, we believe our feelings are the entirety of who we are—and we assume we're unique. Peter identified with his negative feelings. Because everyone else surely had perfect parents and homes, he had to hide the fact that he was "different." This gave rise to shame—because of which his thoughts and emotions had to be hidden. As a result, Peter's personality was unable to grow. Such fixed childhood images may not make rational sense to an adult; but until we release them, they will keep conditioning and karmically binding our lives because they are frozen in the unconscious mind.

As children, we are all very self-centered. We have not fully developed the ability to empathize with others. Simply put, we are happy when we get our way and unhappy when we do not. Many of us continue this emotional trend as adults! This is because we have yet to free the fixed images that cause our immature behavior.

FALSE BELIEFS

False beliefs are fixed generalizations about ourselves and others and our world. They stem from the fixed images of self that form as a result of unresolved incidents that usually occur in childhood. These fixed images of self are always accompanied by false beliefs and feelings of inadequacy. These feelings of inadequacy give rise to twisted patterns of behavior as we desperately try to compensate for our "deficiencies."

We all have belief systems. And if we look carefully at them, we see that our belief systems are mostly designed to reinforce our own ego structure. We identify who we are with our possessions, position in society, thoughts, ideas, and beliefs. The ego is no more than these identifications.

As we practice meditation, we begin to notice that the thoughts and the feelings arise within a space that is larger than the thoughts and feelings. The eighteenth-century Japanese Zen Master Hakuin wrote in his "Song of Zazen (Meditation)":

> From dark path to dark path,
> We've wandered in darkness.
> How can we be free from the wheel of suffering?
> The gateway to freedom is awareness in meditation;
> It is beyond exaltation, beyond all our praises.[6]

We have moments or even long periods of time in meditation when we just notice our thoughts and feelings. As a result, you might realize that the commentary that is always running in your head is not who you are.

False beliefs are not wrong in themselves. We adopt them to cover an inner wound that is now part of our unconscious mind. Until we find and heal that inner wound, we will unconsciously rotate around the same pattern of behavior. This unpleasant repetitive behavior is how our body and mind tell us we have an unconscious wound that needs healing. When our fixed images emerge into awareness, false beliefs and the subsequent deluded attitudes dissolve on their own.

True change only comes from within. To get to the root of fixed images and distorted patterns of behavior, we don't have to analyze or psychologize. But we do need the nonjudgmental awareness we cultivate through meditation and a willingness to get to know ourselves at the most intimate level.

One of the main reasons that I (Shinko) started to practice meditation was because I noticed, through the years, that my mind had become busier and busier, to the point where I didn't have a moment of peace. I was completely neurotic and never in the present moment. I was constantly projecting my own interpretation of reality onto the past or the future. Then I read, in *The Three Pillars of Zen* by Philip Kapleau (my first Zen teacher), that the mind could be trained through meditation. Peace and silence could be restored. I started meditating regularly. As my mind quieted down, I began to see the false beliefs and the accompanying emotions that shaped my life. They are easily accessible through the Great Heart Way, right below the layers of noise and chatter of the undisciplined mind.

A Checklist of Feelings and False Beliefs

The following list contains what are in our experience the most common feelings and false beliefs that emanate from fixed images.[7] You will recognize many of them in the stories in this book. This list can help you develop the awareness you need to recognize your own patterns.

- **Feelings of Abandonment:** People with fixed images related to issues of abandonment or loss could have the false belief "People will leave me."

- **Feelings of Deprivation:** Children who are neglected usually form fixed images related to some kind of deprivation—emotional (lack of love and affection) or physical (lack of clothing, food, school supplies, etc). Their false belief could be "My needs won't be met."

- **Feelings of Subjugation:** Children who grow up in families where one or both parents are very dominant could develop fixed images of subjugation and the false belief "My needs never have priority."

- **Feelings of Mistrust:** Children who are abused emotionally, physically, or sexually usually develop fixed images related to mistrust and the belief "I can't trust anyone," or "I cannot depend on anyone."

- **Feelings of Being Unloved:** Some children grow up in families that use love as a weapon of punishment. Their parents may say, "You did this wrong, therefore I no longer love you." These children feel unloved and their fixed images center on this. Such images can also develop in children of divorce. Children who feel responsible for divorce often hold the false beliefs "I'm not lovable," or "If I were lovable, my father (or mother) wouldn't leave me."

- **Feelings of Exclusion:** Fixed images centered on exclusion come about in children who feel excluded at home or in the first years of school. A common false belief is "I don't belong."

- **Feelings of Vulnerability:** Children who experience a catastrophic event could form fixed images of vulnerability. Catastrophic events usually bring issues of loss: the loss of someone or something they love; and the loss of wealth, good fortune, or material possessions. The most common false belief is "Something terrible is going to happen."

• **Feelings of Failure:** Children whose parents are never satisfied with their performance can develop fixed images of failure and the very common false belief of "I'm not good enough."

• **Feelings of Perfectionism:** Children whose parents only approve of them when they are the "best in show" can develop fixed images centered on perfectionism. A common false belief is "I have to be perfect to gain approval."

• **Feelings of Entitlement:** Children who are spoiled and given everything they want, without having to do anything to earn it, may develop fixed images related to entitlement. Common false beliefs are "I'm special, so I can do whatever I want" and "The rules don't apply to me."

DELUDED ATTITUDES

Submission, aggression, and withdrawal[8] are the three basic deluded attitudes that a child can adopt to compensate for false beliefs and fixed images. These attitudes are "deluded" because they are adopted in ignorance, springing from images we don't even know we carry. As expressions of our hidden karma, they can exist alone or in combination—usually with one predominant *modus operandi*. And since they are almost never examined, these deluded attitudes continue into adulthood.

The Submissive Attitude

In his story (given earlier in this chapter), Peter is a good example of someone with a submissive attitude. Peter had hoped to compensate for his hateful thoughts by "being perfect." Without even knowing it, he decided not to rock the boat. By being completely cooperative and passive, Peter hoped that everyone would find him perfect and not see the hatred he carried inside.

The Aggressive Attitude

With this attitude, we adopt a strategy of superiority and aloofness which, we hope, will protect us not only from our own disturbing emotions but also from the criticism of others. For example, another of our students, Jamal, realized how very hard he was on himself and others. While meditating on the root of this behavior, an image came to him: "I was about five years old, running around the house with a sheet tied around my neck like a cape, singing *'Here comes Superman!'*

Sitting with this image in meditation, Jamal asked himself what underlying belief formed during this seemingly innocent, playful behavior. Then he realized that at a very early age, he had unconsciously decided he *had* to be Superman. His parents had just divorced, and he thought he had to be "perfect" so they would both still love him.

This could have developed into an attitude of submission, but instead it became one of aggression. Jamal realized that he had built up anger as an adult, resenting the fact that he could not fix everything. Projecting this anger onto others, he was critical of their imperfections. Continuing to try to be perfect, even though he knew it was impossible, he caused suffering for himself and those around him.

The person with an attitude of aggression is always trying to be superior, to dominate, to "win." This false self-image demands an independence from feelings that is not humanly possible. Life is constantly proving to this person that he or she cannot live up to this ideal of perfection.

The Attitude of Withdrawal

In contrast to the submissive or aggressive person, the person who adopts the attitude of withdrawal finds relief by retreating from inner problems and consequently from life itself. In the previous chapter, for example, we saw how I (Shinko) couldn't accept happiness. My belief was that happiness was dangerous, and I would withdraw from any situation that threatened this belief.

Underneath our withdrawal, the mind is still split. But as long as circumstances allow, we are convinced we've attained true serenity. Many experienced meditators fool themselves and hide behind this false façade. Yet when life's storms touch them, the inner conflicts emerge and the shallow nature of this false serenity is revealed.

It is common for people to be attracted to Zen meditation because they think that they will become invulnerable to the ups and downs of their feelings. They think that this can be accomplished by developing a deep state of meditation and becoming aloof, cold, rigid, and impassive. This is a misunderstanding. The only way to become invulnerable to our upsetting feelings is to fully accept them and feel them. Then we can be serene and peaceful.

The Power of Nonjudgmental Awareness

To be enlightened does not mean that one feels nothing or only feels bliss all the time. We tell our students, "To be enlightened is to be completely alive and vulnerable, to wear no masks or pretenses, and to be as flexible as a young willow tree that is transparent to the wind." Abiding in our heart is the way to be like this.

To discover how the three deluded attitudes manifest in us, we need constant awareness. By expanding our awareness of life and connecting with our hearts, we can observe our patterns and emotions without being drawn into the drama. We can get in touch with our deeper

being and find a safe space where our identity isn't derived from deluded attitudes. The observing mind frees us from our habitual ways
of behaving.

We need to be especially careful that when we unmask *one* of these
deluded attitudes, we don't reinforce one of the other two. To solve a
submissive problem, for example, we might decide to become more
aggressive. Or, if we realize we have an aggressive attitude, we might
suddenly become more submissive or simply withdraw. The sudden
adoption of a different deluded attitude doesn't solve anything; it only
reinforces the vicious cycle of delusion.

We must always rely on our nonjudgmental awareness. When we
notice that we are adopting one of these deluded attitudes as a response to a specific situation, we need to be aware of it. Just being
aware will help the pattern to dissolve. These patterns are like ghosts
that can only live in the dark. The moment we bring the light of
awareness through the heart-mind connection to them, they dissolve.
We can keep asking ourselves, what will be the most honest way for
me to act in this particular situation? Will this action bring peace to
myself and others? Will it create suffering for me and others? Equanimity comes from our state of being and does not depend on the
events in our lives. The tenth-century Chinese Zen Master Ummon
said "Every day is a good day."[9] Shishin's teacher Maezumi Roshi ex-
panded and clarified this quote by saying, "Even having difficulties,
every day is a good day."

We all want to live our lives with awareness and to work with our
life situations in a fresh, spontaneous, and appropriate way. But we
can't do this while we're still operating out of delusional attitudes that
we are not even aware of. To some extent, the attitudes that we formed
to protect us as children were effective at that time or we wouldn't
have adopted them. But now they only cause an endless cycle of problems and pain. The only way to end this cycle is to unveil our fixed

images and false beliefs. Then we can enjoy the abundant freedom and energy that naturally emerge.

It is common to hear adults blaming their parents for their misfortunes in life. But if we want to heal our karma, we must take responsibility for our own actions and their consequences. When we reach a certain level of spiritual maturity, we realize that regardless of whatever has happened in the past it is our task in the present to solve and to heal. The words of the Japanese Zen Master Torei Zenji, who lived in the eighteenth century, are very clear in this respect:

> *Even though someone may be a fool, be warm and compassionate toward him. If by any chance he should turn against us, and become a sworn enemy, and abuse and persecute us, we should sincerely bow down with humble language in reverent belief that he is the merciful avatar of Buddha who uses devices to emancipate us from sinful karma that has been produced and accumulated upon ourselves by our own egoistic delusion and attachment through countless cycles of time.*[10]

Torei Zenji encourages us to acknowledge that those who seem to be acting against us are really helping us to work out our negative karma. Everything is grist for the mill if we have the right attitude.

A PARENT'S STORY

The following story was written by Tenko Nishida, the founder of a Buddhist service community, Ittoen, in Japan in the last century:

When my son was thirteen, he dearly liked playing cards and became quite skillful. During the winter vacation, he would go around the neighborhood and sometimes not return home until morning. My former wife was very worried and said to me, "He comes back late every night and takes no notice of my scolding. Will you please take him in hand and admonish him?"

I replied, "Sometime ago I might have done this but I cannot do it now."

She protested, "But if we leave him to his own devices, he will be ruined. I am desperately anxious."

"I am anxious too," I said, "but I do not know what to do because I cannot correct even my own errors. For all I know, he also may be trying to reform himself. If I were not ashamed of my own wrongdoing, I might find fault with our son. But as it is, I simply cannot do this. I must first get rid of my own flaws. I am in a very embarrassing position."

My wife was not satisfied, but the only conclusion I came to was that before I could reprove others, I must first become perfect myself. However, I could not help but be concerned about my son's bad habits. Then one day it happened that he came to me with a book and asked me to explain a certain passage, as he was going to give a talk to some children in the neighborhood. I asked him to sit down. I told him how his mother had said I should reprove him for the bad habits he had formed.

I went on, "I cannot do as she asks, because I am unable to change my own bad habits. Although I admit that if I have to wait until I am perfect myself, then there is every reason to be very anxious about your future. I am not qualified to educate you. I am very sorry about this, but it cannot be helped." My son remained silent but his face was sour.

I continued, "If you were to say to me, 'Please point out my faults even though you have faults yourself,' then I should do as you asked to the very best of my ability. If, however, you thought it unreasonable that I should reprove you because I have my own faults, I would not do so. But I should then ask you not to call me father anymore." As I spoke, I unconsciously put my hands on the floor to bow before him. My son seemed to be very annoyed, although he said nothing. Perhaps he had pierced my state of mind, which may have seemed strange but was also tender. The next moment he got up suddenly and ran away. I said to myself, "He's only a child after all."

The next morning I found a letter on my desk addressed to me but bearing no signature. It read, "Please pardon me and tell me about my faults even though you may have many of your own, and please let me call you father." Tears came to my eyes. I called my wife and said, "Read this."

She said, "He was sobbing in his bed last night and seemed to be writing something, I suppose it was this."

Since that time, although I have never spoken to my son in a voice demanding obedience, he has never disobeyed me. But I noticed that he was not so obedient to his mother. The difference arose because I prayed that light would show me my faults, but my wife did not. There is a vast difference between these attitudes. The first seeks to have one's child brought up by light; the second tries to accomplish this by human power. Most parents think there is no other way but to scold a child. No religious teacher or educationalist ever suggests the possibility of a parent frankly acknowledging to his child his own errors, but a new awareness leads me to practice this.[11]

Since Tenkosan practiced from the heart, he was in touch with the depth of his feelings and was able to help his son. When we act from our heart, we touch the heart of others.

MEDITATION AS JUST BEING

Even though our ego identity is fully formed at puberty, we are continuing building barriers and defining a small territory of "who we should be," because we think we can easily control it. But instead we become a prisoner of our own ego. Meditation provides us with a doorway out.

If, as children, we hadn't derived our identity from our mental phenomena, they would have just passed—their nature is transitory. But when the mind attaches itself to thoughts, feelings, images, beliefs, and memories, we solidify them. Unconsciously we identify ourselves with these frozen creations and take them to be who we are. By forming an identity, we actually perceive ourselves as objects, while ignoring our most intimate experiences. Ego identification is an immature form of self knowledge—but it's the best we can do as a child.

As adults, most of us are caught up in our ego attachments the majority of the time. We believe that our dichotomous thoughts, feelings, actions, and opinions that divide the world into self and not-self are the true reality. When our consciousness is anchored in ego identity, we cannot experience reality as it is. Instead we're buffeted around by contradictory streams of recurrent feelings and thoughts, like leaves in a high wind. We cannot see that our true being emanates from our hearts as boundless compassion and clarity.

Our dissatisfaction with life is reinforced by our constant judging, ignoring, and rejecting of all uncomfortable, painful, or anxious experiences. Rejecting these aspects of ourselves divides us internally and prevents us from experiencing the true unity of mind. Our deeper realities are so constricted that we're suffocating in our web of stories, beliefs, and behavioral strategies. Cut off from our true infinite nature, we suffer.

In meditation, we can see how our mind grasps onto passing thoughts, feelings, and perceptions—usually clinging to the pleasant ones and rejecting the ones we dislike. And we see that grasping and rejecting is a vicious cycle, a dead end that goes nowhere. At first, we try to do something with these thoughts, feelings, and perceptions: we reject them, fight them, or attach to them. But when we learn to let go of thoughts and feel with our heart during meditation as well as in daily activities, we experience moments of silence, peace, spaciousness—and just being. *Between* our thoughts, something unknown and wonderful starts to happen.

The experience of maintaining our heart connection in each moment can precipitate a spontaneous transmutation of old energies. Just feeling the energies of envy or jealousy with our hearts, for example, can transmute them into clarity and compassion. This transformation opens us up to a deeper and wider view of reality, a view that is grounded in our hearts.

In meditation we learn to accept, tolerate, and love our inner space. When we stop reinforcing thoughts and are able to dive into our feelings, the larger dimension of our being unfolds before our eyes.

Viewing from the heart can heal old wounds from the past by connecting us, in a more compassionate way, with the original situations and people involved. Old wounds then reveal hidden treasures. In the places we've turned away from, we discover the deeper qualities of our being. Thus healing old wounds brings forth something new.

The importance of meditation to Great Heart Way cannot be overstated. Unless you learn to discipline your heart-mind and to pay attention to your thoughts and feelings without judging, you will continue to be trapped in twisted patterns of behavior. Traditional Zen training has tremendous value, but it does not explicitly teach how to transform these patterns into compassionate action. As we mentioned, it is possible to bypass personality issues in traditional meditation by entering a deep, almost trance-like state. But the issues return when the meditator returns to his or her daily life. At our Zen

Center, our students are encouraged to follow the Great Heart Way and to enter the realm of the heart in order to develop emotional balance and compassion.

EXERCISES

The following exercises offer ways to find clues to your hidden images. The best clues are found in the repetitive patterns of discomfort in your life. When discomfort and emotional pain arise, connect with your heart and stay with the pain. Don't look for your hidden images. They will be uncovered by bringing awareness to your feelings, and by staying with them without judgments or stories.

Before doing the following exercises, it is again recommended that you meditate for at least twenty minutes. Then carefully read the exercises and reflect on them throughout the day. Always maintain your heart-mind connection and keep writing your responses to the questions in your journal.

1. Do you remember your early hateful feelings, including hateful feelings toward yourself?

2. What are your early memories of feeling guilt?

3. Do you remember childhood thoughts of not being loved enough and/or feeling that others were loved more than you? What conclusions did you draw about not being loved enough?

4. Can you recall any behavioral strategies that developed to compensate for what you perceived as a lack of love?

5. What standards do you set for yourself to make up for what you perceived as your faults?

6. Which one of the three deluded attitudes—submission, aggression, or withdrawal—did you primarily adopt?

    a. How do traces of the other attitudes manifest in your life?

    b. How do you use each of these attitudes? What role do they play in your life?

    c. What are you hiding behind these attitudes?

    d. How would you approach your life without depending on deluded attitudes?

7. Ask your closest friend what she or he considers to be your virtues and faults. Put these in two columns: virtues and faults. Watch your reactions, but do not try to change them and do not identify with them. Record how you felt when you received this feedback.

5

RELEASING FIXED IMAGES

I want to unfold. I don't want to stay folded anywhere, because where I am folded, there I am untrue.

—RAINER MARIA RILKE[1]

As we mentioned in the previous chapter, a memory becomes a fixed image when, as children, our immature minds encounter situations that are too complex or emotional to deal with. These incidents cause a shock and leave an impression in our young minds. This impression is reinforced by a mental picture of the incident and a wrong conclusion or belief. When that happens, all memories of this event—mental, physical, and emotional—spontaneously retreat into our unconscious mind, forming a fixed image.

When I (Shinko) was thirteen years old, my father died in an accident. I loved my father so much. When I heard the news, I remember I just became immobile. I don't know for how long; it could have been seconds, minutes, or even longer—and then I acted as if nothing had happened. My unconscious circuit breaker had gone off. I put my reaction to my father's death into the deep freezer of my unconscious mind. I couldn't work with such strong feelings at that age, so I unconsciously postponed my grieving for many years. I first grieved for my father's death when I was in my thirties.

Until these kinds of unprocessed events are dealt with, the immature attitudes of our childhood dominate parts of our adult mind and behavior. Many of our present difficulties are rooted in unconscious childhood logic and trapped in fixed images. (Later in this chapter we will see different ways these fixed images can form.) The re-enacting of childhood patterns gives us a clue that energy is obstructed in some area of our body. Becoming aware of these patterns allows us to undo them.

Behind every seemingly stuck and unchanging behavior pattern, a fixed image is at work. For example, when we consistently attract certain kinds of events or people that create problems in our lives, we can be sure that a hidden image is controlling our behavior.

When Celia was nine years old, her parents moved from Chile to Peru. At her new school in Peru, Celia's classmates treated her like an alien and made fun of the way she spoke and wrote. Celia felt ashamed and told herself, "I am an alien girl and I will never belong." As time passed, this statement retreated into Celia's unconscious mind. Now wherever Celia goes, she tries to fit in but always carries the unconscious fear of not being accepted. This fear of rejection has manifested as a fear of having close relationships, causing Celia to behave in unfriendly ways around people that she likes. As a result, people see her as cold, distant, and sassy, and keep their distance. Her unconscious belief of being an alien keeps being confirmed. This is one example of how hidden beliefs and images could become self-fulfilling prophecies.

Another indicator of a fixed image is a pervasive sense of shame, a feeling that we're not worthy or deserving. A specific shame harbored in our inner child comes from the shock of discovering our parents and our world weren't "perfect." It can arise when we first discover that we're not perfectly loved, or when we're treated badly. As children, we assume this is our fault. We don't know other families well enough to compare them to ours. By the time we understand that no one's parents are perfect, the shame is already deeply rooted and self-esteem is handicapped.

SOPHIE TRANSFORMS FEELINGS OF INADEQUACY

Here is what Sophie discovered during a seven-day meditation retreat, during which she focused her practice on recurring feelings of inadequacy.

First, I just sat in meditation with my emotions. My initial feelings of inadequacy shifted to feelings of rejection. I felt intense tension in my chest, which made my breathing difficult. I remembered to connect with my heart and the tension eased off. Then the following image emerged.

I was twelve years old, and I was leaving my ballet studio with my good friend Laura. My dad was walking from his car to the studio and he greeted my friend: "Hello Laura. I haven't seen you in a while. You're looking good. I wish I had a beautiful daughter like you, instead of a plain-Jane like my Sophie."

I didn't hate my dad. I was just devastated, flattened, crushed. We got in the car and drove off. I said nothing to him. Now I sat totally immersed in this overwhelming sadness, feeling every drop of the misery. Since I was also a forty-six-year-old, safe and sound on my meditation mat, I could really live through it. When the bell rang, I felt like I had thrown up: the kind of throwing up that makes you feel really glad to have thrown up, because it releases so much toxic energy from your body. I felt emptied out and very clean.

I thought I was finished with this image. But when I related the sadness and purging feeling to Shishin Roshi in private, he hit me with the next step: "What did the twelve-year-old tell herself? What conclusions did she draw from this experience?"

I went back to all that sadness and tried to remember what I was thinking at the time. The old thoughts were still there for the finding. Sophie the twelve-year-old told herself that she was right. She had always suspected her father didn't care for her looks, her brains, or her very existence. His remarks had just proved it. She was not good enough; she should have been a boy.

That still wasn't the end of the process. Shinko Sensei suggested I go back to the "devastation" and give that girl what she wanted or needed. I felt skeptical about being able to do this. I felt it would be exhausting to go back into the sadness for a third time, but I was curious enough to try. I was already so astounded by what had been uncovered, I didn't care if anything else happened. So, without really knowing how this works, I went back through the entire memory again.

After we drove off, I yelled and screamed and swore at my father, until I burst into tears and begged to know why he didn't like me. I told him how bad it hurt that he thought I was ugly. My dad stopped the car and put his arms around me. He said that he was so sorry, that he was surprised that I didn't realize he thought I was the most beautiful girl in the world, and that he loved me so much. He apologized for saying that my friend Laura was more beautiful than me. He said he just wanted to be sure that I didn't become as proud and arrogant as my friend. He was just teasing my friend. I was exactly what he wanted.

For most of my life I've struggled with a lack of confidence. It seems these behaviors were all self-inflicted. As an adult, and

*especially as a parent, I have come to appreciate all the won-
derful and unselfish things my father did for me. I consciously
realized that, not only did he love me very much, he was actually quite proud of me.*

*Lately, I find that I don't respond in the same ways to certain
situations. Receiving a simple compliment, for instance, I'm as-
tonished to find that instead of immediately denying my worthi-
ness, I actually believe the person who compliments me. I just
feel grateful. And this gratefulness seems to arise from a "blank
page"; whereas the unworthiness came from a page cluttered
with lists and formulas for how to behave. At times, it's uncomfortable not being able to fall back on old habits. But I don't really mind or worry about it too much. It is quite a freedom.*

Like many of us, Sophie had adopted a pattern of denying and
burying her feelings. To protect ourselves, we become insensitive to
pain and conflicts. Becoming numb to ourselves, we become equally
numb to the feelings and pain of others. Thus we can watch others
suffer without feeling any discomfort. This body-mind state causes
much of the world's wars.

In the case of child abuse, children are generally unable to recognize destructive behavior in protectors and caregivers. They rationalize any harm done to them and conclude that it's their own fault. This
false belief harbors a secret shame. Children then numb their feelings
as an unconscious defense against being hurt again. While children assume abuse is their fault, they also sense that something's wrong in the
family and that certain people can't be trusted. These conflicting parts
of their worldview work against each other, making it very difficult
for children to bring the truth out into the open. Consequently, parts
of their personalities cannot develop.

Our adult feelings of shame or disappointment are symptoms of
hidden childhood images and can be used to reveal these images. If we

fully feel our old repressed pain when it comes up, we can ask ourselves, "Where does this pain come from?" Then the light of awareness
can penetrate the fear, resentment, and shame that we experienced as
children.

Dr. Alexander Lowen discovered that he had to let go of his ego attachments to get in touch with his body feelings. In his book, *Joy*, he
recalls:

> *The way to recover my integrity and give the courage to follow my*
> *chosen path [was to] surrender to the body. What I had to surren-*
> *der was my identification with my ego in favor of an identification*
> *with my body and its feelings.... Surrender to the body would in-*
> *volve giving up this inflated ego image which covered and compen-*
> *sated for underlying feelings of inferiority, shame and guilt.*[2]

This is a part of our passage into adulthood: bringing our original
disappointments to awareness and re-experiencing old hurts, anger,
and resentment. Until we deliberately make this passage, we will keep
re-enacting childhood patterns.

JOSÉ BECOMES THE POOR BOY

Although José came from a middle-class family, he realized
that his view of his life was permeated with a sense of poverty
and shame. He often felt that he either didn't have enough or
he had less than those around him. This sense of poverty controlled his interactions with others. During meditation he became aware of his feelings of poverty and uncovered a fixed
image from his childhood.

Where José grew up, there were very poor children who had to sell things to survive. They were called *maniceros,* or peanut-sellers, because this is mostly what they sold.

One day when José was walking down the street, he turned a corner and came face to face with a manicero—and they were both wearing the same shirt! It was a red and blue striped T-shirt. Both boys stood there in shock. In José's mind everyone else disappeared; he and the manicero were alone on that street. They stared at each other without saying a word.

Seeing this poor boy in an identical shirt shattered José's sense of being middle class. As the boys parted ways, he felt ashamed, humiliated, and poor. As soon as he got home, José took off the shirt and never wore it again. From then on, however, he felt he had less than others. Although his family was still middle class, inside he felt very poor.

Having found the incident in which his sense of poverty was frozen, José could allow thoughts of poverty to arise and vanish without identifying with them. Thoughts of poverty no longer condition or obscure his interactions with others. When the wound is healed, the scar has no power.

José explains, later in this chapter, how he deprogrammed this fixed image.

When we liberate ourselves from fixed images, we become more fluid and adaptable, acting and speaking in accordance with circumstances. To do this, we must pay attention to our minds and our lives. We must learn to see how reoccurring events and circumstances—so easily dismissed as coincidence or cruel twists of fate—point to what is hidden. When we locate what is hidden, we are no longer bound by what formed long ago in response to circumstances no longer occurring. Then we can respond to life with spontaneity and wisdom.

The following example demonstrates how a belief formed in childhood conditioned the subject's adult behavior.

JANE'S INABILITY TO EXPRESS HER NEEDS

> Jane's mother didn't want to spoil her when she was a small child, so she decided not to pay attention to Jane when she cried. But she did pay attention to her at other times. This created an impression in Jane's mind to which she attached the following belief: "In order to have my needs met, I should not show my emotions." The combination of the impression and the wrong conclusion created Jane's fixed image, which continued to condition her behavior as an adult. Jane went through life unfulfilled, because she never expressed her needs. Awareness of this recurrent pattern helped her to find and recover from the long-forgotten fixed image.

A fixed image can act like a strong gravitational force in the center of a microcosm around which specific patterns of behavior form and attract negative events to our life that seem to occur without our doing anything to create them. The price to be free from the influence of this inner microcosm is awareness—and the willingness to see and accept without judgment what is within us.

REVEALING FIXED IMAGES

A hidden image can only be found by tracing the feelings and thoughts that emanate from it and recognizing the patterns they form in our life. In other words, we work *with* the symptoms, not *on* the symptoms. This means approaching the symptoms—the habitual thoughts, actions, and underlying feelings of discomfort—with an open, totally accepting heart.

Sometimes these feelings of discomfort are quite vague, but you need to pay attention to them. This murky sensation in your body, which could be an indication of something unresolved, is also an emotion being born. It cannot be born directly into the light of consciousness without you feeling it first. Once it is felt, the brain will recognize it and give it a name. Avoid imposing words on your feeling as it forms. Let it arise with its own essence and identity.

Please note that you should not try to remember all of your childhood memories—this misinterpretation is a common mistake. Fixed images are not regularly part of our conscious memory, but there certainly are exceptions. These exceptions consist of old memories that keep coming to our conscious awareness because they need to be healed, as in the example of Albert in the next chapter. If conscious fixed images exist, the usual way we access them is by being mindful of the memories that frequently pop into our awareness.

In the majority of cases where fixed images are unconscious, we can access them by directing our awareness toward the symptoms, as in the following example. For Grace, a forty-year-old nurse, the symptom that guided her to a fixed image was the repetitive bubbling up of the thought that other people's feelings were more important than hers.

GRACE'S FIXED IMAGE

For quite some time I have noticed that I repeatedly think that other people's feelings are more important than mine. I decided to take a chance and explore that thought. When I connected with the bodily sensation associated with it, I felt the pain of sadness. Then I had feelings of being let down, betrayed, and overpowered. I just felt the pain behind those feelings, and the following image suddenly burst into my memory.

My mother's grandparents lived in northern California when I was a little girl, and we would visit them on occasion. One time, Grandpa gave me a fascinating little stamp box. I was overjoyed and I ran to show it to my mom who was in the kitchen with Grandma. Mom hustled me out of there, telling me I absolutely could not take it home. Shocked, then furious, I started to cry. Then she told me to stop crying and be nice, so I wouldn't hurt Grandma's feelings.

When I asked myself "What did I say to myself at that time?" the answer came to me very clearly: "My feelings don't matter. And if I'm going to be a good girl, there are feelings that I am not supposed to have."

In meditation, as I reflected on this image and my wrong conclusion, I became full of hatred for my mom. I immediately shut that down—but I was aware of shutting it off. I tried again to stay with that hatred, so I didn't have to carry it any more. What I then found was a swarm of memories: so many times, I had felt hatred and turned it off, denied it, or turned it into something else.

Then a huge wave of hatred welled up in me. I hated my mother for taking the box and shutting off my feelings. I hated my dad for how he treated my mom. I hated Shishin Roshi and Shinko Sensei for making me feel all this. It is not possible to accurately describe how consumed I was by hate. Just trying to remember it to write it down is making me shaky.

What happened then was entirely unexpected, but absolutely perfect. Connecting with my heart, I experienced all that hatred as a big balloon, with a tiny pinhole in it. And slowly it just vanished. I felt so light I thought I might float. Now, two months later, I still feel like a backpack full of rocks has fallen off my shoulders. I didn't realize I was carrying such a burden until it fell off.

When Grace noticed her repetitive thought of "other's people feelings are more important than mine," she decided to explore it. Repetitive thoughts or feelings that keep bubbling up in our unconscious mind give us a clue that there is something buried beneath, which is calling out to be released. What Grace did next is a very important step in releasing the fixed image: she did not make a story about her feelings but just connected with her pain. When Grace recovered her lost memory, she asked herself as a little girl, "What did I tell myself at that moment?" She concluded, "My feelings are not as important as other people's feelings. And if I'm going to be a good girl there are feelings that I'm not supposed to have." When Grace recovered this wrong conclusion, which is a general statement about her world, she reflected on it and observed the ways that it had conditioned her reality as an adult.

In the past, Grace would have repressed her negative feelings by "shutting them off," but this time it was different: she now has begun to develop the skills to work with her feelings. She has her awareness and heart-mind connection. Awareness and a heart-mind connection is what makes this method effective and their power should not be underestimated. Heart-mind awareness in particular functions as a larger container in which feelings can emerge, be known, and effectively be released.

KARMA AND FIXED IMAGES

The negative karma created by fixed images manifests as an inability to overcome certain patterns of behavior, a lack of control over certain events, and a fear and resistance to specific occasions.

Focusing on my fear of happiness that I (Shinko) mentioned at the end of chapter 3, I recalled when some friends gave me a birthday party. I felt my heart racing with happiness, when a sensation of terrible fear started circulating through my body. Excusing myself from the party, I went to a quiet spot in my backyard. I concentrated on my feelings. I was shaking with fear that something terrible was going to happen; I didn't know *what*. I felt like running away and canceling the party, but I didn't. That would have been acting on a feeling, in order not to feel it.

Instead of acting on the feelings, I continued shaking with fear. Suddenly, the fear passed away, and the following image came vividly to my mind. I was about five years old. I had been invited to play at a neighbor's house and I was having a great time. Innocently, I plugged in a TV with a cable strung across the room. Later, I learned that the neighbor's grandmother had tripped on the cable and broken her leg, dying a few months later.

The conclusion I drew from this image was "If I am too happy, something terrible will happen." Thus I conditioned myself to avoid happiness. After finding this fixed image and the false belief I fabricated, I was able to heal and deprogram (neutralize) the image. I transformed the negative karma as described in the section "Deprogramming Fixed Images."

We should not underestimate the consequences of the negative karma trapped in fixed images. Believing that "it's not good to be happy"—a belief that was sabotaging my life—I projected a veil of sadness that clouded my reality and brought into my life people who reinforced the same unconscious beliefs like a microcosm of unfortunate events that gravitated around my fixed image.

The images and beliefs hidden in the unconscious mind continue to project negative situations into our lives. If we're unaware of our shadow, we will feel we're a victim of circumstances. We will blame others for what happens in our lives, denying personal responsibility— and when we deny responsibility we also deny ourselves the power to effect true positive change.

WRATH OF GOD

In the Introduction, I (Shishin) described how I discovered my hidden belief of "I'm not good enough." My healing process continued as I observed this thought whenever it arose: without doing anything about it, I was just aware of it. I dwelled in the awareness of "I'm not good enough," and suddenly the thought transformed into strong feelings of fear. Reassuring myself that the light of my nonjudgmental awareness would guide me, I entered into the unknown and uncharted territory of my mind.

Connecting with my heart, but without making up any stories about the fear, I focused my awareness on it. As I stayed with it, the fear grew sharp and intense. Suddenly, a very old memory of religious school popped to my awareness. It was about how angry Moses was when he brought the tablets with the Ten Commandments down from Mount Sinai, only to find the Israelites worshipping a golden calf. I felt so scared when I first heard this teaching that I had immediately pushed it away.

But that was not the end of it. Focusing on this image, another one arose. It was of Abraham preparing to slay his son Isaac at God's command. Isaac was saved when a ram appeared tangled in the brush, and God commanded Abraham to sacrifice the ram instead of Isaac. From that story I had formed a strong belief: "If you're not good, they'll kill you!"

I could see clearly the origin of my false belief about not being good enough. And I could see that the terrifying fear accompanying this belief was trapped inside me all these years. It was truly "a matter of life and death." Isaac was about to be killed and he was a good boy. What would be the fate of an imperfect child such as me? I thought, "I'll never be as good as Isaac, and they will kill me for sure."

Because of that unexamined belief, I've spent my life trying to prove to others that I am good enough. All hidden beliefs carry negative karma. Looking for the approval of others so I wouldn't "get killed," I betrayed my true feelings on many occasions. This caused problems, unhappiness, and suffering for myself and others.

To completely heal this unhealthy belief, it wasn't enough to see its origin. I had to undo the negative program imprinted on my mind by the fixed image. I did talk with a knowledgeable Rabbi about this image, and he gave me sophisticated Talmudic explanations that clarified things somewhat. But those explanations would never satisfy the inner child. To free myself from the negative karma I was carrying, I needed to deprogram the fixed images. I was able to do this by comforting the frightened child as discussed later in this chapter.

CHARLES OVERCOMES A PATTERN OF FAILURE

In this case, Charles, a thirty-five-year-old computer programmer, relates how he healed an old belief that had on many occasions sabotaged his success.

During walking meditation at a Great Mountain Zen Center retreat, I realized I had a nagging sense that I was doing something wrong and that others were criticizing me. Of course, since the retreat was held in silence, this was pure conjecture. And I began to realize this feeling did not just come up in retreat. I felt this way all the time. I was living with a tightness in my chest and shoulders that was so constant I wasn't even aware of it—until I had the chance to sit a few periods of meditation.

Still, I said to myself that such a subtle feeling surely couldn't lead to anything more than some small irritating belief. My expectations were low but, I was determined to work through the emotions and do the exercises.

Sitting in meditation, I was aware of the physical sensation of the tightness in my chest and shoulders. Memories of playing cards and checkers with my father came back. I had always felt the same uneasiness and physical symptoms then. That was the key: being aware of the physical experience. My mind was only too happy to go off track, analyzing and rationalizing. In past work, that's what I would have done—and that's as deep as I'd get.

I remember Dad mocking me for always losing at checkers. (Of course, a six-year-old probably would always lose to an adult.) And I realized that he wanted me to lose! Over the years he taught me to be a loser. Being aware of the physical sensation, however, I didn't feel this was what it was about; although it does go a long way to explain my vague, lifelong sense of failure.

After feeling the tightness in my chest and shoulders, some apparently unrelated memories flooded back. For many years my father would come home drunk every Friday night. An argument with my mother would inevitably follow. He would then storm out again, leaving her in tears and crying that he'd kill himself while driving—and leaving me feeling completely powerless. I now realize I formed the belief that if my mother or I contradicted or challenged him in any way, he would leave and possibly die.

This belief spread to every area of my life. I sabotaged my education; after all, he had only completed tenth grade and may have been threatened by my success. I'd wanted for many years to start my own business, but never followed through; several businesses that my father started were unsuccessful. I'd won a scholarship to the Naval Academy and went into the officer training program. But after a few months, I started drinking heavily and going AWOL. Eventually I was discharged after a drunken prank involving shoplifting. The flash of insight I got was that my father was an enlisted man. For me to become an officer would go against my belief that I couldn't best him in any way.

The Great Heart Way gave me the combination of tools I needed to heal my fixed image and the microcosm of karmic

*events that it attracted. For the first time, I could go deeply into
the physical symptoms of old beliefs while maintaining a nonjudgmental, witnessing awareness. The wonderful thing is that
clearing my false beliefs of failure led to even deeper meditation experiences and allowed me to strengthen my motivation
to continue along that path.*

Charles realized that his meditation experience was more profound
when he dealt with some of his personality concerns. When our personality is not addressed as part of our spiritual path, our unresolved
personal problems become a hindrance to our spiritual progress. In
general terms, we could say that our personality represents the relative
mind, as compared to the absolute or infinite mind that transcends the
personality. In the Buddhist verse *Identity of the Relative and Absolute,* it
says that the relative and absolute mind are interconnected "like the
foot behind and the foot in front in walking."[3] If we only work with
the absolute mind and leave behind the relative personality, it is like
trying to advance with only one foot. We can still make some progress
but it cannot be compared to having both feet moving freely. Working
with our personal issues as part of the spiritual path allows the ego to
merge with our infinite heart–mind.

RECOGNIZING THE BASIS OF BEHAVIORS

How can you know if your behavior is based on a fixed image and
false beliefs? First, pay attention to your thoughts and feelings in the
present moment. Are they proportional with and appropriate to the
present situation? When a car cuts you off in traffic, is your anger appropriate or is it excessive? When your partner misunderstands you,
do you feel slightly upset or completely crushed? How do you feel
when you're with other people, particularly new acquaintances?

We should always question our reactions. When they are out of proportion in relation to a particular event, it gives us a clue that there is a fixed image at work.

RASHIDA OVERREACTS

Rashida was criticized at work by a co-worker. She noticed that the criticism was not so harsh and that she could have taken it lightly, but somehow she couldn't. Instead, she felt completely devastated and had thoughts of quitting her job. Since she was aware that her reaction was disproportionate to the event, she decided to take a closer look at what was going on. Connecting with the pain underlying her feelings of devastation, she found hopelessness and more pain. Feeling her pain without trying to make stories about it, Rashida suddenly remembered a time in her childhood when she overheard a member of her family criticizing her. Rashida felt crushed and from that event, she drew a conclusion, "People don't see the real me." She felt hurt and hopeless. These feelings, the wrong conclusion, and the incident in which she was criticized by a family member, formed the fixed image that retreated into her unconscious mind. Now every time she feels criticized, the same feelings of hopelessness and devastation bubble up to the surface. They give Rashida a clue that there is something inside her that needs to be healed. If we want to heal our fixed images, it is of crucial importance that we observe the appropriateness of our reactions to each situation.

Emotions are natural and healthy and are not to be suppressed. But emotions that are disproportionate to a given situation provide a valuable clue that you're operating from an outdated belief system. When brought to awareness, these old beliefs can be released. Then you can experience things as they are, freed from the weight of conditioning.

I (Shinko—chapter 5) found an image, when I noticed my feelings of guilt as I was about to have a good time. Peter (chapter 4) found his image when he noticed his submissive behavior in order to get love and approval. Jamal (chapter 4) noticed the anger and resentment toward himself and others. Jane (chapter 5) noticed the fear she felt of exposing her true feelings. Jose (chapter 5) noticed that thoughts of poverty were conditioning his life.

Once your fixed image has been identified, the next step is to begin to release it. Everyone has more than one fixed image, but we work with them one at a time. Fortunately, they also manifest one at a time.

RELEASING A FIXED IMAGE

To release a fixed image, we must connect with our heart and feel all of our emotions thoroughly, without trying to interpret them and without creating stories in our heads. We all have such images, and so we all have to deal, on some level, with similar categories of feelings. If we believe we're alone and different from everyone else, this belief is a symptom of the prison we have built for ourselves.

When we lead Great Heart workshops, everyone feels a wonderful sense of relief in discovering that we all secretly hold similar feelings and thoughts. They were kept hidden because we thought that we were different, that others would ridicule us if we exposed these secrets. As adults, it is liberating to find that our hidden feelings are shared by everyone in the group. We are not, after all, so different from anyone else.

We need to be tolerant of our disturbing emotions. We don't have direct control over our thoughts or feelings—but we can control what we attach to. Doing this takes effort, perseverance, and practice. For example, in Grace's story, she was aware of having feelings of hatred.

Just being aware of them gave her a larger container in which the feelings could manifest and then dissolve. This would not be possible if she allowed the feeling of hatred to influence and define her sense of personal identity. The negative karma we've created tends to be self-perpetuating; but by shifting the tendency from identification to simple *awareness,* we can break the cycle.

It takes a lot of effort to undo the karmic consequences of our unwholesome actions. It takes *atonement.* Just admitting a wrongdoing or inappropriate action is not atonement. True atonement has to include grieving due to the harms we have caused. Grieving, in turn, means deeply feeling the pain associated with the offending action. In the beginning, we may feel like we're swimming upstream! But when we shift from attachment to awareness, the spiritual path of inner growth and transformation is much easier. It is like swimming with the help of the current.

Crying and Grieving

Some of us have found that on occasion when we open to our fixed images and to our distorted patterns of behavior we feel an intense need to cry and grieve as the old unfelt pain trapped in the fixed images come into consciousness. If this need happens to you, it is very important that you allow yourself to cry and weep. It will pass and it will bring to you a new sense of who you are becoming. The snake changes its skin, the old tree grows a new shoot, the new blossom opens up.

When we recover old fixed images of times when we were victims of abuse, we can release the old stagnant pain by crying out. This is a way to allow the pain that we had carry inside us since we were children to leave the body. After we cry we will feel clean inside with a new sense of transparency. This is the same process that naturally happens in nature when the dark clouds can no longer hold their heavy weight of moisture and rain falls to the ground. The drops of rain purify the air and nourish the earth. Please, if this happens to you, do not judge your tears. Just let them flow the way they want to. The same way that the clouds do not judge themselves saying "I should not rain today" or "It's not proper for a nice cloud like me to rain" or "What would the other clouds think of me" or "I am a male cloud and male clouds don't rain." Let us be like nature, spontaneously free, natural and without self-judgments.

On the topic of crying, psychotherapist Tara Bennett-Goleman says, "It can be tremendously freeing to allow the mind to let go and the body to give itself up into this release, as though some inner force knows just how to release the pain…It's beneficial to let such a release happen the way it wants to, completely naturally."[4]

Deprogramming Fixed Images

At this point—having brought a fixed image into conscious awareness and healing the feelings associated with it—we are ready to *deprogram* our fixed image. To deprogram an image, first visualize yourself at the time of the event. Then in this visualization, give emotional, mental, and physical support to yourself as a child: all the support you needed, but didn't get.

Some of the advanced teachings of Tibetan Buddhism are based on visualizations of oneself in remote times and places. It is not just a process of thinking about a memory. You have to feel it with your whole body. Buddhist teacher and psychologist Jack Kornfield writes, "Through imagining and envisioning our inner difficulties, we are able to rework the wounds and struggles, the conflicts of the past…. In using skillful visualization with our heart and mind, we can begin to powerfully transform our world."[5]

Here is how Jamal (from chapter 4) describes deprogramming his image:

As I worked with my image in meditation, I realized that the red Superman cape I was always wearing had become very heavy and burdensome. I visualized myself taking the cape off. I felt light and free when I did this. Then I went back in time, and I took the sheet off the little boy I used to be. I told him, "It is okay to play Superman, but you should know you don't have to be Superman. People will still love you if you are just yourself. I love you just the way you are."

In my own case, I (Shinko) told the little girl who plugged in the TV, "What happened in childhood was just a misunderstanding. It's okay for you to be happy and enjoy life." And I visualized embracing myself as a little girl until she totally dissolved inside me.

José (from this chapter) wrote:

I deprogrammed my image by mentally going back to the time when I felt very poor. I told the boy who I was, "You are who you are and you are not made by the clothes you wear. Your future only depends upon your hard work and your aspiration." I embraced the confused child inside me until he dissolved and we became one person.

Someone once remarked during a Great Heart workshop, "This method of deprogramming the blocked image seems too simple to be effective." It seems simple because this is the last step in the healing process.

The first step is noticing our repetitive behavior and thought patterns. Then we must thoroughly feel our long-standing repressed emotions. The healing process comes to a peak when an unconscious memory emerges into the light of our awareness and when we find the false belief, or wrong conclusion, that accompanies that image. The last stage is deprogramming the fixed image. We have students who have ignored their feelings for so long that they have become numb and cannot even identify simple feelings. When they become aware of this, they slowly begin to notice their feelings in reaction to different events in their life. Once the door is slightly opened, the feelings start to trickle out and later to flow out. In some cases, they flood out. The images emerge eventually, after a student is able to feel his or her feelings.

It is very important to finish the healing cycle with deprogramming. This way we can be sure that old images don't leave any traces behind. Our fixed images are the first manifestation of negative karmic forces in our lives. And so, the first step in healing these traces is to find and release the images. In the following chapters, we will continue to illustrate this healing process, following the steps of the Great Heart Way.

EXERCISES

As always, precede the exercises with at least twenty minutes of sitting meditation practice. Increase this to thirty minutes, if you can. Then reflect on the exercises that follow. If you don't have much time, just do one exercise a day. Record your response in your journal right away; or, reflect on the exercise until the end of the day and record your response then. Be sure to always maintain your heart-mind connection.

We recommend working with your images while sitting in the meditation posture. This posture is particularly helpful because it supports the mind as it concentrates on hidden issues while meditating. You can focus your attention on any images that might have arisen, and ask yourself what conclusion you drew at the time.

1, Look at your behavior patterns, as a child and as an adult. For example, as a child, did you hide your true feelings for fear others would reject you? Did you agree to do things just to please others, even when you strongly didn't want to? Did you try to dominate others to avoid facing your vulnerability?

    a. What patterns do you find?

    b. Can you recall the beliefs that underlie these patterns?

    c. In the present, are you overly assertive or overly passive?

    d. Do you act aloof and superior, as a way to protect yourself?

    e. What makes you uncontrollably angry? What do you most hate?

Write down your observations. Try not to judge yourself. There is nothing "bad" about anything you discover. You are simply learning about things that you've hidden from yourself.

2. Be aware of repetitive and familiar thoughts, feelings, and reactions that cause you discomfort or pain. When you find them ask yourself, "When did I first experience this?" "In what circumstances did this arise in my life?" Feel all the emotions in your body. If you have a moment, sit in meditation and continue to experience your emotions. You do not have to count or focus on the breaths now. Your concentration should be connecting with your heart while you feel your feelings. No matter what arises, allow the feelings to be, without identifying with any thoughts you might have about them. Record your experience.

3. What memories arise, after feeling your emotions thoroughly? If a vivid, old memory appears, this is the image. There might be many layers of unfelt feelings. If you've been emotionally numb for a long period of time, it may take longer to find an image. That's okay! Just feel what you feel,

without any expectations. By doing this work over and over, your body will become sensitive again. Eventually, without pressure, an image will surface in your conscious mind.

4. When an image appears, find the emotional belief and wrong conclusion that arose from it. To do this, ask yourself, "What did I tell myself at the time of this event?" Then write down the exact words you said. If you cannot recall the exact words, just keep trying by asking yourself the same questions until these words manifest to you. The fixed image is trapped within a statement you made a long time ago about your reality and the world around you. In order to liberate the image, you must bring that statement into your conscious mind.

5. Heal the image by visualizing yourself at the time of the event. Close your eyes, sit erect on your meditation cushion or chair. Visualize giving all the emotional, mental, and physical support to yourself as a child that you had needed, but didn't get.

Remember: No matter how long it takes, an image will appear. For some it may take longer than others, but throughout the process you will be getting in touch with your emotions and feeling more alive. It is well-invested time and effort.

6

TRANSFORMING
NEGATIVE KARMA

*It is often tragic to see how blatantly a man bungles his own life
and the lives of others yet remains totally incapable of seeing how
much the whole tragedy originates in himself, and how he continually feeds it and keeps it going. Not consciously, of course—for
consciously he is engaged in bewailing a faithless world that recedes
further and further into the distance. Rather, it is an unconscious
factor which spins the illusion that veils the world.*

—C.G. JUNG[1]

Negative karma manifests in devious and distorted ways. Unbe-
knownst to us, the rejected aspects of our mind interfere with
our plans and hopes for change and growth. On a conscious level, we
may struggle to change negative habits; but our efforts for change are
impeded unconsciously. This is no reason to feel hopeless. The cause of
our lack of fulfillment and happiness in life is right in front of our eyes
and it can be dissolved.

The following example of Albert illustrates this. Albert is a forty-
six-year-old businessman, married, and the father of two boys. His
experience is very important for two reasons: first, he was able to

find the root of his disruptive behavior patterns; and second, his experiences will help you to further understand the steps of the Great Heart Way.

▰▰▰▰ ALBERT FINDS THE ROOT ▰▰▰▰
OF HIS INNER STRUGGLES

For years, I was bothered by persistent and seemingly unsolvable emotional problems. For decades I worked hard to change, but I made very little progress. I was able to live a normal, functional life; but I carried a pain with me that seemed to never go away.

The most dramatic problem was my temper, which I was completely unable to control in certain situations. I would fly into childish rages far out of proportion to the circumstances. Although my temper tantrums left me exhausted, ashamed, and disgusted with myself, they happened again and again. I felt powerless to stop them. My negative tendencies were activated by recurring situations and stresses. Until these tendencies dissipated, I lived under their painful spell.

I spent many years doing self-analysis and introspection to find the causes of my problems. Memories uncovered from my childhood seemed to hold a clue to my behavior,* but being aware of them was not enough to break their hold on me.

When I began the Great Heart Way, I had already remembered my first irrational temper tantrum and its cause. I was about eight years old and was making a model airplane for my

*It is our experience that most of the fixed images are unconscious, but there are exceptions as in Albert's case. See our comments in the previous chapter on this subject. Some of you may have persistent memories from childhood that are not unconscious but need to be healed nonetheless. Until they are healed, they will chase you and create a sense of shame.

father. I often made presents for my mother and father to win their affection. This airplane was about three or four feet long, with the body and wings made of sticks bound with twine. I was delighted with it, and was very proud of myself for being bright enough to make it. I hoped my parents would think it was wonderful.

But at one point I needed some help. I couldn't attach the wings to the body of the plane. I tried repeatedly, but finally I went to my father for help. He was busy with work, as usual, and said he would help me later. After a time, I asked again and was put off once more. Still later when I asked, he said he'd help me the next night. Frustrated and anxious, I awaited his help, but day after day his response was the same. Then one night he got mad and angrily told me to quit asking him.

I went back into the basement and, in desperation, decided to finish the plane by myself. I tried, but it was too big to hold; the more I tried, the more messed up it got. Tears poured down my face. Eventually my frustration boiled over into rage, and I took the plane and smashed it to pieces against the work table. Finally Dad came downstairs—and I got in trouble.

I had remembered all this before, and it did seem to hold clues to my temper. My temper tantrums were never directed at people, always at things, like my poor airplane. They happened frequently when I was working alone and felt frustrated by not being able to complete some task. But seeing and understanding this connection didn't stop the actual tantrums. I was still liable to throw my wrench across the yard when trying to change a spark plug. I can't begin to describe how bad this made me feel about myself.

Following the teachings of the Great Heart Way, I traced my feelings back to the memory. [See chapter 5, exercise 3.] Since I had already recovered the fixed image, I put myself into the boy I had been and allowed my body to feel what he felt. And

*what I experienced was not rage but sadness, despair, and re-
jection. I felt like crying and had a sinking heaviness in my chest
and body. I felt drained of energy, ignored, and unimportant.
My rage was covering all that up so I wouldn't have to feel it.*

*I then tried to articulate the false conclusion I'd believed as
a child. [See chapter 5, exercise 4.] It came right to my lips:
"Nobody cares about me. Dad doesn't care about me." When
I did the Great Heart exercises, I saw I still carried that false belief. It was, indeed, one of the motivating factors of my temper
tantrums. I saw that I really do feel desperate and alone in similar situations, burdened by a sense of deep despair and hopelessness. My temper tantrums were a way to avoid dealing
with that.*

*In doing the Great Heart practice, I saw that the shame I'd
been carrying around for so many years was a very heavy burden. It now became clear to me that this memory had a huge
amount of energy connected with it.*

*In completing the last part of the practice—offering my
childhood self all the help and support he wants—I was amazed
by a couple of things. First, this former self was very much alive
and active inside me. It breathed the same air I did, and I could
easily connect and give it real support. This showed me that the
past is not out of reach and unchangeable; it is alive right now.*

*The second thing was the amount of relief and release I felt.
It was huge—just opening a dialogue with this part of myself,
and telling the child I'd help him anytime he needed it. A vision
came to me: I was pulling a knife out of my heart that had been
buried there for thirty years. I realized I had experienced a persistent pain all these years, which I just ignored until I didn't know it
was there anymore. Letting go made me feel a thousand pounds
lighter.*

*I doubt that I've suddenly solved all my emotional con-
flicts, but I feel like I've taken a real step in that direction.*

More importantly, I finally have tools to apply to the problems that were impossible to grasp before.

This morning I sat with the image of my father again. Suddenly I saw him as I had when I was seven. I was amazed at the pure and uninhibited love and admiration I felt. He was the biggest, strongest person I knew, and I took it for granted that he could never fail at anything he did. I had lost that feeling over the years, building many walls between us to protect myself from disappointment. I was always slightly on my guard around him. To see my father again with seven-year-old eyes was a very pure feeling. I treasure it. It makes me think about my boys, too.

CREATIVE AND DESTRUCTIVE STREAMS OF MIND

To thoroughly understand the unhealthy processes that take place in our minds, we need to acknowledge our "streams of mind." In the Great Heart Way, we recognize the existence of a creative stream and a destructive stream of mind. The creative stream includes everything we label as positive: *Yes,* life, love, creation, gain, and pleasure. The destructive stream includes everything we label as negative: *No,* death, hate, destruction, loss, and pain.

When we speak of different streams, we do so to elucidate the two forces that result from the split in our *one* mindstream. The destructive stream is not intrinsically harmful but, due to our ignorance, we use it in a harmful way. When we understand the origin of this destructiveness, we can release it.

The following account of Lulu clearly illustrates these two streams of mind and the inner war of "good" versus "bad."

GOOD LULU AND BAD LULU

I've been struggling with behavior issues all of my life. I would often be completely unaware of my negative behaviors. I'd seem to be "at fault," but wasn't sure why. This terrified me at times. People reacted in negative ways that mystified me. I knew there was something wrong, but I didn't see how I contributed to it. I found myself apologizing to people without knowing what I was apologizing for. This caused me to feel awkward, confused, and ashamed. It deepened my feelings of helplessness, worthlessness, and despair of ever being able to enjoy time with other people.

I tried being very, very careful around people. I studied how to behave and trained myself to be aware of group dynamics and personal interactions. I took courses in conflict resolution and how to deal with difficult people. I tried psychotherapies and metaphysical healing practices. I finally came to meditation practice to see if the peace one supposedly experiences would help. But nothing really worked.

During a Great Heart retreat, a lost memory flashed into my consciousness. I was a small child, maybe two or three years old, and I was inside the cupboard where mom stored the linens and towels. Using a stepping-stool, I had climbed up into this cupboard intending to be a "big girl" and help mom fold the towels. It was so delightful being in this space with all the soft, clean, cushy things around and under me. I was really enjoying it, when mom showed up.

I can only imagine what the linen closet looked like! Mom asked, "What are you doing?"

"Nothing," I said.

"Who did this?"

"Bad Lulu did it."

"Where is Bad Lulu?" she asked.

"I don't know."

"Who are you?"

I said, "I'm Good Lulu."

She asked me these sorts of questions over and over, but very gently. I think she was concerned that I was lying or perhaps creating another identity.

A "split" clearly did manifest in me at this time. I already knew the concepts of good and bad. And I could only be good, I could not be bad. Somebody else did the bad stuff; I did the good stuff. If I had done whatever my mother was asking about, I wasn't going to admit it, not even to myself. Even at that early age, I had seen what happened to people who admitted doing bad things and had probably experienced it myself. In our family, violent retribution was the norm. I've blocked much of that out of my memory. If you did something bad, you got hurt; even if you did something bad and didn't know it, you got hurt.

I took this image to my private interview with Shinko Sensei and shared it. I knew there was more there, but I didn't know what to do next. Shinko Sensei suggested I recover "Bad Lulu" and let her out of my shadow. She told me that because "Bad Lulu" was still in my shadow, she was expressing her power in a negative, destructive way.

I knew that at times I purposely did things to hurt people— and felt some small sense of enjoyment in the moment. But afterward I'd feel remorse. When I internally criticized and punished myself, "Bad Lulu" felt even worse. She needed to express herself! And she would then express herself in twisted ways, by hurting people, over and over and over.

Shinko Sensei told me that "Bad Lulu" is not bad per se; she is really a representation of my power. And it was essential to acknowledge and release "Bad Lulu," so that my power could help me. I need my power to do this work. I need my power to be effective in life. I need my power to really take care of my-self and others. "Bad Lulu" was my power to cut off, to set boundaries, to protect, to preserve, and to play. I am still dis-covering exactly what this power is and how to use it.

I have the tools to heal my problems and the willingness to do it. I feel a confidence that I didn't have before. And I'm not afraid to go back into my heart and feel what I need to. Fear still arises, of course, but it is not incapacitating. It's just an-other feeling that dissolves in my heart.

VICTIMS AND PERPETRATORS

Some fixed images relate to the times we felt like victims; some relate to the times we felt we were perpetrators of suffering. Both victim and perpetrator images carry negative karma, because their energies are stagnant—and energies that don't flow become toxic. But fixed "per-petrator" images are the more painful and difficult to heal. It takes a lot of courage and a big, accepting, open heart to bring awareness to the suffering we have inflicted on others.

I (Shinko) had healed many fixed images from times when my in-ner child felt like the victim of circumstances. Then I started becom-ing aware of images of myself as the perpetrator. A particularly painful image came to mind of the time I threw my aunt's dog over the fence. As a child I had small white mice as pets. I cared for them and played with them every day. My aunt, who lived with my family, had just been given an adult dog. One day, I came home from school to find that the dog had opened the cage and killed several mice. As I held their bodies in my hands, tears fell down my cheeks and I felt tremen-dous grief that turned into fury. I took the dog to the backyard and threw him over the tall fence. Since then I have been burdened with remorse and guilt.

I did not know how to heal this image. Nothing seemed to work. I tried to deprogram it by talking to the girl I was at that time. I told her I was very sorry about what happened to her pet mice, but that it was not okay to inflict pain on the dog. Educating my inner child in this way seemed to help, but it did not release the charge associated with the event.

Usually the first fixed images that we recover relate to occasions when we were the victims. As we release these images, additional ones of ourselves as perpetrators might start to emerge. The same Great Heart Way techniques apply to these images, but the main difference is that they need a lot more healing than those when we were the victims. First try deprogramming a "perpetrator" fixed image and the pain surrounding the particular event associated with it by giving the child what you think he/she needed. In my case I acknowledged her pain but I also educated her. If the pain does not go away, there is more karma that needs to be healed. This pain is like a sore in the heart and it comes to our conscious mind with a thought such as, "I am sorry I threw the dog over the fence" or just simply the memory of throwing the dog over the fence. As these thoughts or memories continue to come to mind, we can easily connect with the pain underneath. This pain, although it is easy to access and connect with, could also be easy to repress. It all depends on what you want to do with it. If you repress it, it will always be there.

When the pain persists, I find it most helpful to ask your body directly what you can do to heal the pain. Restrain yourself from using your brain and your analytical faculties to provide an answer. Allow the answer to emerge from your body. Stay a while in the unknown. An answer in the form of pictures or words will arise in your conscious mind. By trusting this process, you are trusting your inner wisdom.

When I asked myself how to heal the pain I felt from hurting the dog, a series of thought-pictures came to my mind in sequence. I saw how I take special care of my fifteen-year-old dog, Hobbes, to ease the pain of his old age. I saw myself taking care of him with nearly the tenderness I would give an aging relative. I saw how when it is cold outside, I put a warm coat on him because his body cannot take the cold very well anymore. I saw myself giving the same intensive care to his meals and to cleaning up after him when he makes mistakes in the house. I remembered how a friend saw me caring for Hobbes and said, "What good karma your dog has." Unconsciously I said, "Yes he has a very good karma, and I have a bad one." This sequence of thought-pictures came to mind when I asked myself how to take care of my inner pain. I realized then that I have been unconsciously re-pairing my old transgression by taking care of my aging dog in such a way. With this realization, my inner pain dissolved.

We are not sharing this process with you in order to tell you that you have to try to figure out a punishment for your wrongful actions. Healing is not about imposing anything from the outside. It is about asking your body to tell you what the hurt is about and hearing from your body how to heal it. The path to healing our perpetrator faults will be different for each one of us.

For example, about forty years ago while living abroad, I (Shishin) had a female cat who had a penchant for getting pregnant. Being young and poor and carefree, I did not have her spayed, and had to find homes for all of the kittens. After a half dozen pregnancies, and being at my wit's end, I decided to kill one litter of kittens. I mentioned it to a friend who was in a meditation group with me and he could not be-lieve that I could do such a thing. I was so ashamed at what I had done that I could not tell anyone about it, including my family. I suffered in silence and relived the heinous crime in my mind many times. I dreaded telling anyone about my crime. I was not able to discharge the guilt I felt even when I felt the pain and prayed for forgiveness. Finally in a Great Heart retreat I confessed to the participants what I had done. I said, "I am a killer and I had not told anyone for forty years because I was so ashamed." I was amazed to find that by sharing my dark secret, the cloud of ignominy lifted. In fact, a number of people in the group admitted to abortions and other acts where they had taken life. It was liberating for all of us. Now I can talk about that unfortunate event and work with the karma I created.

BEYOND TIME

Both quantum physics and Eastern "mysticism" view time differently than most of us do from our ordinary reality. The Buddhist scholar and practitioner D.T. Suzuki wrote:

> *In the spiritual world there are no time divisions such as the past, present, and future, for they have contracted themselves into a single moment of the present where life quivers in its true sense.... The past and the future are both rolled up in this present moment of illumination, and this present moment is not something standing still with all its contents, for it ceaselessly moves on.*[2]

Although our rational, conscious mind is attached to the belief that past, present, and future occur separately, the unconscious requires no such concept. The fluidity of time is also explained by physics. When I (Shishin) was studying physics at the University of California–Berkeley in the 1960s, I and my colleagues had the most precise experiments to show that time could flow either forward or backward in the microscopic world. The principle is still valid today, and many physicists have spoken about it in philosophical terms. The pioneer Erwin Schrödinger wrote, "There is no before or after for mind. There is only a *now.*"[3] Thus, it should not be surprising that we can actually *heal past karma* as though we were experiencing it in the present moment.

In the process of spiritual transformation, it's crucial to treat our inner perpetrator with compassion. Saint, devil, victim, and perpetrator are just one mind. Zen teacher Bernie Glassman holds meditation retreats at

Auschwitz, Nazi Germany's largest concentration and extermination camp. There they focus on healing the suffering of both the victims and perpetrators.[4] Jesus said, "Let him who is without sin cast the first stone." (John 8:7) We do share the same mind of the worst criminals because essentially there is only one mind. As Stanislav Grof wrote, "I saw clearly that humanity's problem is not the existence of vicious dictators, but this Hidden Killer that we all harbor within our own psyches."[5] When we accept and heal the perpetrator within, we can do much to help others, because we can emanate to them the same understanding and compassion we have been able to extend to ourselves.

The main difference between a criminal and a person who has never committed a crime is that the criminal gets attached to his destructive and negative thoughts and feelings. A non-criminal can detach from those thoughts. Through the nonjudgmental awareness developed in the Great Heart Way, we can stay present with our worst thoughts and feelings and allow them to dissolve on their own. We have seen the positive results of traditional meditation for those in prison, and through our work with prison chaplains we know that the Great Heart Way can effectively address criminal impulses. This practice is safe, as long as we're aware. When we're aware of terrible thoughts and feelings, our awareness is already larger than they are. Terrible thoughts and feelings can arise and vanish into that space.

THE EVIL WOMAN

I (Shinko) came face to face with the unconscious destructive aspect of my mind the day I visited a psychic healer. I don't know exactly what he did; I only remember entering a state of supreme bliss. When I got home, I went to lie down to enjoy this blissful state.

In a state between sleeping and wakefulness, I suddenly had a terrifying vision. An evil woman with bloody eyes came out of my own body, grabbed me by my throat, and tried to strangle me. For a second, I was able to stare in her face and was shocked to discover the evil woman was none other than me: me in my meanest imaginable manifestation. The moment I tried to liberate my throat from her grasp, she vanished inside my body again.

I felt very scared after this experience. The only thing I thought to do was to carry salt around with me, which I had heard prevents witches from appearing. Before I went to sleep, I threw a lot of salt around my bed. Feeling somewhat ashamed of this frightened behavior, I decided to tell my Zen teacher the next time I saw him.

A few days later, I went to a retreat and told my teacher what had happened to me. He asked, "Didn't you say you were in a state of bliss before you had that experience?" I said, "Yes, I was." He then replied, "You left her out! Manjushri's sword has two sides—good and bad—but it is only one sword!"

Manjushri is the *bodhisattva* (compassionate, enlightened being) who represents wisdom. He is often depicted carrying a sword, which has two edges: one for giving life and the other for taking it away. On the spiritual path, we have to die to our delusions and attachments—that is the death-giving edge of the sword. Then we are reborn to a life unencumbered by petty fears and desires—that is the life-giving edge. If we leave out one edge—whether it is good or bad, right or wrong, life or death—then we are incomplete, since together it is one sword.[6]

The evil woman represented all the negative aspects of my (Shinko's) mind that I denied and pushed out of my awareness. Negative energy is not bad or evil in itself. Only when it's pushed "underground" and kept hidden in the dark does it become constricted in our body-mind and turn against us. I had felt the energy of the evil woman inside me on many occasions, but I never took it seriously until I learned about the shadow-bag we all carry.

You don't need to go to a psychic healer to have an encounter with your destructive energies. Destructive energies are at work in your life at this moment, trying, in devious and distorted ways, to confirm false beliefs and fears. They continuously try to surface in the conscious mind. You can recognize and heal them by connecting with your heart and by being aware of your thoughts and feelings.

Recently a Jungian analyst was explaining how fairy tales can help us to understand how destructive energy works when it's ignored.[7] In "Sleeping Beauty," the king and queen invite all the fairies to attend the celebration of Princess Aurora's birth—all but one. The wicked fairy, Carabosse, is not invited. And so Carabosse puts a curse on Princess Aurora. This is what our own destructive energy does when it's not acknowledged: it works against us like an unconscious spell.

Keeping our destructive energy hidden from ourselves makes us weak, frightened, and insecure. When our negativity is out in the open air, we can use that liberated energy as part of our creative power. And we can use it to liberate hindrances from our life. But this doesn't mean we become utterly passive, completely subject to the will and wants of others. Without feeling insecure or confused, we can use our liberated energy to say "No" when we have to say "No." As my Zen teacher taught me, by recognizing the evil woman inside me, she and the blissful woman were able to merge into one indivisible energy—like Manjushri's sword.

Integrating Streams of One Mind

Through awareness and guidance, we can free our energies so they can flow again as one. Destructive energy can be used in creative ways to cut off things that are harmful or obstructive in our life. If, however, destructive energy is used to bring us pleasure, then it is not available for useful and creative purposes. Later in this chapter, we will talk more about the power created by liberating our destructive energy.

The next case illustrates how when our negative energy is attached to the experience of pleasure, it becomes harmful to ourselves and others.

THE CASE OF THOMAS, A SPIRITUAL LEADER

Thomas is a spiritual teacher who damaged his community with his sexual promiscuity and abuse of alcohol. Using the Great Heart Way, he was able to transform his negative karma and behavior. The first step in this process was the discovery of an old fixed image, from the time he was about seven years old.

A memory entered his awareness of hiding in the brush with a girl he liked. Thomas and the girl were touching each other in a sexual way, when he was called to come into the house. When he was asked by his mother what he was doing in the brush, he lied: "Nothing." He then associated the negative behavior, the lie, with the positive feeling he gained from the sexual experience, crossing his negative and positive energies. As an adult, Thomas was unfaithful in marriage, but he never acknowledged his sexual improprieties. He always seemed to himself to be the victim of circumstances rather than the perpetrator of this behavior.

When he started to follow the Great Heart Way, Thomas clearly saw his pattern of attraction to forbidden sex, which had emerged from his fixed image and resulting false belief. When the old memory of hiding in the brush and lying to his mother came to his awareness, he realized he had told himself at the time: "Sex must be secretive, and I must lie about it in

order to survive." The negative karma trapped in both the image and belief caused a lot of hurt and damage to the people
in his community, his family, and himself.

REPRESSION OF THE NEGATIVE STREAM

When we are ignorant of the fact that the positive (or creative) and the
negative (or destructive) streams comprise the essential energies of the
universe, we may choose to reject, repress—but secretly enjoy—our
destructiveness. Then the mind's creative and destructive streams begin
to interact in unhealthy ways that fuel negative karma.

▦ TYLER'S HATRED FOR HIS PARENTS ▦

When Tyler was three years old, he was sent to his room and
told to sit in a chair because he had been "bad." With this punishment, many feelings arose in Tyler's body-mind: feelings of
sadness, rejection, and also hatred—and he didn't have a clue
how to work with them. What could he do in order to survive
this situation? Because he didn't know how to deal with his
pain, Tyler felt hatred for his parents. But hatred didn't alleviate
the pain. Like many of us as children, the only remedy young
Tyler found was to start feeling good about a negative feeling,
in this case, hating his parents. (As adults we call this rationalizing, defending, or justifying our actions.)

When Tyler was released from his punishment, he wanted
to inflict pain on his parents. One trick he had learned was to
hide in the closet until he heard his parents say, "Where is
Tyler?" Then he would stay in there as long as he could, so that
his parents would miss him and regret punishing him. Later in

life, he continued this behavior by rejecting, criticizing, and intimidating anyone who did not fulfill his desires.

Remember the example of Thomas: he started feeling good about forbidden sex at a young age. By crossing his positive and negative energies in this way, he became addicted to lying and to forbidden sex. Normal sex was no longer attractive to him. On the other hand, when we allow our mind to be free, without blocking, avoiding, or denying its negative aspects, they will naturally release themselves. By abiding in awareness, we can watch our destructive tendencies without judging, condemning, or acting on them. By doing this our destructive energies will naturally blend with our creative forces and become one indivisible energy of compassionate wisdom that can spontaneously give or take away according to each situation.

HEALING THE NEGATIVE STREAM

When negative feelings arise in our body, we just connect with our heart and feel them without claiming ownership. The thoughts bubbling up from the unknown depths of our minds are manifestations of universal energy. When we think "I hate that person" or "She is so ugly and despicable," we can simply be mindful of those thoughts, acknowledging that they are present without thinking they're "mine."

When we observe thoughts without identifying with them, thoughts pass like clouds drifting in the sky. We call them "thoughts without an owner." In the same way, we allow our destructive mindstream to surface so that it can merge with our creative mindstream. We do this by connecting with our heart and feeling our emotions without creating storylines. Remember that feelings are just the body's energy currents. Realizing this, we begin to undo our numbness and unify our streams of mind.

I (Shinko) discovered the destructive mindstream trapped inside me the day I decided to buy a house. When I started the buying process, I experienced an acute and disturbing fear. I remembered then the words of the poet Rainer Maria Rilke: "Fears are like dragons that guard our deepest treasures."[8] I told myself that the greater the fear, the bigger the treasure. With the determination of a treasure hunter, I decided to stay with my fear no matter how long it lasted—which was actually only a few hours.

The feeling of intense fear caused my body to shake all over. By connecting with my heart and not making up any stories about my fear, I experienced it in a new way. The actual sensation became like charges of electricity inside my cells. But rather than causing me harm, they were filling my body with new life. When the charges passed away, renewed peace and clarity filled my body and mind. I experienced exactly what Rumi described: "In the poison, there is the elixir."[9]

Then a fixed image came to my awareness. As a child I was very mischievous, and one day I angered my uncle. In order to control my behavior, he told me that I'd never succeed in life. The fear of never succeeding in life was too scary for me to handle at the time, so I pushed it into my unconscious mind. As a result, it became a negative, destructive energy that later sabotaged my wishes and creative efforts.

As an adult, whenever I felt that unconscious fear, I just put a tight lid on it and rejected any situation that might cause it to surface. I rejected, for example, invitations to go to Asia, because the adventure might not be a success. But this time, I clearly saw that the amount of fear I felt by simply buying a house was disproportionate to the situation. My fear was there for me to feel and not repress. Had I not stayed with my fear, I'd have never discovered the fixed image nor brought my negative mindstream into awareness—and, of course, I wouldn't have bought a house.

When the negative stream of mind is freed, it naturally merges with the positive stream to become one energy. The destructive stream itself is not right or wrong, healthy or unhealthy. It is the unawareness of our destructive energy that makes it harmful. Free and unblocked negative energy is a part of our intrinsic strength and power, and can be used in constructive, creative, and positive ways.

GETTING PLEASURE FROM NEGATIVITY

When as children we suffered some strong impression (remember the examples of Thomas and Tyler in this chapter), a specific process took place. To protect ourselves, the positive stream of mind was used in a distorted way in order to alleviate fear, shame, or hurt. Thomas started to feel good about lying and having forbidden sex. Tyler felt good about inflicting punishment on those who disapproved of him. As children, of course, we don't know we have one stream of mind. And we don't know how to deal with "bad" feelings toward ourselves and our parents. When Thomas was caught in the brush, he wasn't sure how to deal with shame. So he began to lie in order to protect himself. Submerging the feeling of shame, he identified lying with feeling good.

As a defense, we push away our original negative feelings and superimpose positive thoughts on the hurt, fear, hatred, or shame. Thus, by trying to protect and help ourselves deal with the situation, we learn to take pleasure in negativity. We learn to take pleasure in lying, revenge, anger, hatred, envy, jealousy, and so on. Taking pleasure in these unwholesome actions entangles our karma and brings suffering to ourselves and others. Like Thomas, we imprint our mind with a negative program that binds our actions as adults.

To state this in another way: as children, burying the negative aspects of our personality may have been the best we could do to survive in a world we didn't quite understand. Now, as adults we can undo those old patterns of behavior and live creative, open, and fulfilling lives.

Unfortunately, many adults continue to be attached to the pleasure of indulging in negative actions and thoughts. There are always occasions when the misfortunes of others make us feel good, redeemed, or self-righteous. Gloating when the sport team we dislike loses a big game is a relatively harmless example. A more insidious example is the pleasure we take when our enemies are killed in war.

Attaching positive value to negative energy short-circuits the mind. To understand this, we can use the analogy of electricity. To turn on a light bulb, the negative and positive poles must complement each other without interference. Then we have light. When the positive pole crosses with the negative pole, we have a short circuit and darkness. The same principle applies to our mind. Unfortunately, when we cross the poles in our mind, it generates an attachment to negative pleasure that then becomes habitual. The seventeenth-century Japanese Zen Master Hakuin called it our "habit-ridden consciousness"[10] and said that it is the biggest impediment to self realization. Like a drug habit, that attachment creates dependency. Thomas became dependent on lying and forbidden sex. If positive pleasure were not attached to negativity, there would be no dependency or addiction.

Our negative karma is entangled in layers of fixed images and wrong conclusions. In order to get what we want from life: good relationships, self-knowledge, enlightenment, a joyful life, etc., it is imperative that we take a deep look at what our feelings are about. Our negative karma is fueled by fear. Usually, unless people have been trained in how to work with fear, they run away from it. This running away from fear prevents deep transformation, healing of childhood traumas, and letting go of fixed belief systems that prevent us from living a more fulfilling life. As we previously mentioned, fear sometimes conditions us to reject what we most want, subtly manifesting in ways that seem to confirm our wrong conclusions. Fred provides us with another example of this.

FRED FEELS HE CAN'T BE TRUSTED

Fred's hidden belief is that he is inadequate and can't succeed. This inner conviction causes him to behave in ways that, indeed, seem inadequate. Moreover, he fears success, because his inner conviction makes him feel he couldn't live up to success. During meditation, Fred was able to find this fixed image.

The image is of himself at about seven years old, being sent by his parents to the neighborhood store to buy some groceries. To his chagrin, when he gets to the store he finds he has lost the money. When Fred returns home, he is told that he can't be trusted. The idea of not being trusted is a very painful one. As a defense, Fred seeks pleasure and safety in this belief of untrustworthiness. The belief becomes unconscious, and being untrustworthy comes to feel good and safe because of Fred's early programming.

As victims of circumstances, we can't find fulfillment in life. It is possible—by exposing our destructive mindstream and its consequent behavior—to see that we lack success because, deep inside, we've decided we can't succeed. We must rescue our negativity from the hidden areas of our mind. Negative karma is fueled by fixed images. When we release an image, we are on the path to releasing its negative karma.

If Fred could have accepted the pain of not being trusted, this feeling would have dissolved. But Fred was only a child who, like most of us, couldn't yet work with his feelings. As an adult, he ran away from every risk. Instead, he could have said to himself: "Look! The fear is here again. Let's see what this fear is about."

In meditation, Fred learned to experience the bodily sensations of fear. He commented, "Hey, this isn't that bad. It feels a lot like excitement; it feels cold; it feels like being alive!" Some readers may think that Fred is converting his aversion of fear into attachment to new states of arousal. If that were so, he would be trapping himself into another fixed state. But as long as he employs nonjudgmental awareness and his heart-mind connection when adopting his new approach to feelings, there will not be danger of getting stuck again. It is not like seeking for thrills and excitement from the fear of something like bungee jumping. Attachment to the thrills of fear doesn't happen in the Great Heart Way because as we feel the fear completely, it dissolves and takes us into what was underneath—such as pain, other feelings, a memory, or a boundless experience of genuine compassion. Instead of attachment, we develop a willingness to look into whatever arises. The labels of what people usually call "good emotions" that we want to feel versus "bad emotions" that we don't want to feel start to fade away. Simultaneously we develop a sense of equanimity.

Truly experiencing fear without a storyline allowed Fred to go deeper. Then the old image burst into the light of awareness, and Fred felt the pain of not being trusted. Experiencing this feeling with his whole heart transformed it into a feeling of deep sadness. And then the sadness opened up into boundless joy.

This is not always as simple as it may seem. Feelings do not always transform quickly from one to another. The only way to pass through this transformation is with the heart-mind of unconditional acceptance. We must be willing to stay with our pain, our sadness, our anger for as long as the bodily sensations last—whether it is hours, minutes, days, or weeks. Only then will they have enough space for the natural transformation to occur. We can't just think "I've been sad for an hour and nothing has happened. This isn't working!" Such an attitude will not be helpful.

In meditation we cultivate the mind of "not knowing." This means letting go of control over our feelings and entering the mind of the unknown. We do not know how our feelings will transform or how long it will take. But when we let go of control, there are no expectations and time no longer matters. Paradoxically, this lets things unfold more quickly—but this can't be our main motivation. In his masterpiece

Siddhartha, about the quest for truth of a fictional contemporary of the Buddha (who bears the same given name as him), Hermann Hesse wrote that when this seeker, Siddhartha, was asked what he knew how to do, he replied: "I can think. I can fast. I can wait."[11] We usually want quick solutions to problems and dilemmas. When we learn to be patient and bear witness to our joys and sorrows without seeking a "solution," the solution appears in ways that we least expect.

Fred healed his old image by visualizing himself at the time it formed. He told the young Fred: "When you were little, you couldn't accept the feeling of not being trusted. But I'm a grown man now, and I can accept all my feelings no matter how negative or frightening they are. Don't worry, little Fred, I'll take care of you now." And the child Fred dissolved inside the adult Fred—thus changing the old program and transforming the negative karma.

Our deeper being manifests when we can observe without judging. Fred was able to reveal his negative karma by throwing away all notions of good and bad, right or wrong. His hidden beliefs were revealed. He understood that he lacked success not because he was inadequate but because, deep inside, he believed he couldn't be trusted—and he feared any event that would put that to the test.

To release fixed images and negative karma, we look first at those layers that are easily accessible to us. These are the repetitive thoughts, feelings, and actions that are almost second nature, and easily overlooked. We bring awareness to these vague, hazy, half-conscious reactions and question them in that light. Thus we liberate our negative karma.

Negative Energy as Ally

When our energies are unified, our destructive power becomes our ally. We can use it freely to cut off what we don't need in our life. But when our destructive power is entangled with pleasure, it is not really available to us when we need it. Have you ever noticed how people who take pleasure in their destructiveness are unable to cut off their own bad habits or vices? When our energies are filtered through our hearts, the destructive stream of mind becomes of service to our creative power. It then adapts spontaneously to the need to give or take away depending on circumstances, as we mentioned before.

For example, in our meditation center we have many different kinds of students. No one rule would apply equally to all. As the Taoist expression says: "What is right in one case is not what is right in another; what is wrong in one case is not what is wrong in another."[12] Some students we treat nicely, softly, and kindly and this is easy. But there are also situations where a Zen teacher needs to break through a student's dualistic games and manipulations and cut through layers of delusions. If the student is not fully committed to letting go of his or her ego-grasping ignorance, she or he may feel threatened and strike back at the teacher. The student may need to be asked to take time away from the Center or even to leave.

In *The Nicomachean Ethics,* Aristotle wrote: "Anyone can become angry—that is easy. But to be angry with the right person, to the right degree, at the right time, and for the right purpose and in the right way—that is not easy."[13] The liberation of the destructive stream of mind is essential for the manifestation of the spontaneous wisdom that knows when to give and when to take away.

EXERCISES

Preceding these exercises, do your twenty minutes of meditation. If possible, increase the time you spend meditating. Sitting in meditation mornings and evenings will help improve awareness. Even if you can't do this every day, consider doing it sometimes. Then reflect on the exercises and write your responses in your journal.

Some of these exercises require reflection throughout the day. So read them, answer what you can in your journal, and then think about them as you continue through the day. At the end of the day or maybe the next day, write some more in response to these questions. Always remember to maintain your heart–mind connection.

1. What feelings, attitudes, and beliefs prevent you from being satisfied with your life now?
   a. When you are dissatisfied or unhappy, experience the feelings that arise.
   b. Is there a pattern?

2. What do you want to be different in your life?
   a. What feelings, attitudes, and beliefs prevent you from changing?
   b. What is the fear that prevents you from shifting your beliefs?

3. Be aware of destructive *thoughts*. Don't try to shut them down. Just be aware without interfering with them.
   a) Write down significant thoughts that you would ordinarily shut down, but can now allow to be there.

4. Be aware of disturbing *emotions*. Do not try to shut them off. Just feel your emotions without trying to interpret them.
   a) Write down significant emotions that you would ordinarily shut down but now allow yourself to feel.

5. Note when you find yourself feeling good about negative feelings or thoughts, and write it down. Allow yourself to feel the pleasure attached to the destructiveness. You must be very

aware of this. Then you can allow your mindstream to reconvert itself.

       a. What are the consequences when, for the sake of mo-
          mentary satisfaction, you give in to destructive im-
          pulses?

       b. What choices do you make as you observe the de-
          structive attitudes and intentions within you?

       c. Record the times when you cross your positive and
          negative energies.

       d. In what ways does this destructiveness manifest? How
          does it affect your life?

6. When do you notice your positive mindstream responding to
positive events?

7. When do you notice your negative mindstream responding to
negative events?

7

THE GREAT HEART PRACTICE

To go through life with a closed heart is like taking an ocean voyage locked in the hold of the ship. —ALEXANDER LOWEN[1]

The worst prison would be a closed heart.
—POPE JOHN PAUL II[2]

N ow that many of you have started to cleanse your system of outdated beliefs and fixed images, it is time to make another step into a more advance meditation that will continue opening up your life to a greater expanse of joy, peace, and compassion.

BREATHING THROUGH THE HEART

In contrast to the first meditation practice we taught in chapter 2 [where you concentrate in the *hara* (lower abdomen) area], with the next practice you rest your concentration in the area of your physical heart.

You can practice this meditation in the sitting posture described in chapter 2 or while in activity. If you are practicing sitting down as you breathe through your nostrils, visualize the air filling up your heart area before it descends into the hara. Then exhale normally. Practicing this meditation while in sitting posture will allow you to strengthen your heart-mind connection and to purify your thoughts and emotions. The heart filters ego delusions much like a water filter removes water impurities.

You can also engage this practice at any time and in any place during your daily activities. Functioning from the hara tends to cut off interactions and communication with others, while functioning from the heart opens up connections. We can take our heart-mind connection with us when we stand up from our meditation cushion and go into the world. When our awareness is connected with our heart, the dualistic mind loses its power. The ego cannot survive in the heart. Just accept whatever is taking place. Allow each experience to be, just as it is, free of judgment and totally transparent.

Pema Chodron wrote,

> *If your everyday practice is to open to all your emotions, to all the people you meet, to all the situations you encounter, without closing down, trusting that you can do that—that will take you as far as you can go. And then you will understand all the teachings that anyone has ever taught.*[3]

Of course, this may sound simple; but it is an advanced practice that can require much preliminary practice and commitment. That is why we teach it after you have developed concentration in your hara and have opened your heart to some extent. You will undergo a period of trial and error. For example, when you are standing in the supermarket, at the bank, or at work, you can watch your discriminating intellect take inventory of people around you: "That one is too fat," "That one is too short," "That one looks angry." Without fighting this discriminating mind, just peacefully return your concentration to your heart. Then something wonderful and almost miraculous happens: you see those people as they really are. You see their perfect nature. Our egotistical discriminating mind looks for faults; the heart, when it is open, sees everything with compassion. The heart sees the heart in others. When you see human beings from the heart, you will recognize others as your own self; your own self is everyone else.

Based on research by Gary Schwartz, professor of psychology at the University of Arizona, and Linda Russeck of the Heart Science Foundation, psychotherapist Stephen Harrod Buhner says, "The heart can act as a 'mind' or an organ of perception because approximately 60 percent of heart cells are neural cells, which function similarly to those in the brain.... By learning to locate consciousness in the heart, we begin to know the world—mineral, plant, animal, and human—in a way that is long forgotten but most natural to us....When we locate consciousness in the brain, we reduce the breadth of full perception and thought to a narrow band. Everything else is relegated to the realm of superstition and heresy. But when we reclaim the heart as an organ of perception and cognition, we feel first and then we know the oldest way of being human."[4]

The essential practice now is to be able to maintain a heart-mind connection *in the midst of* thoughts and emotions. It is only our reaction to thoughts and feelings that make them thick and solid. Whether you're driving the car, working, talking, sitting around, or even feeling very disturbed—just bring your awareness to the heart. When we're totally present in our hearts, emotions and disturbances transmute on their own into compassionate wisdom and clarity. We become like the great alchemist who can transform lead into gold.

Maintaining the Heart-Mind Connection

By maintaining our heart-mind connection in the midst of thinking or feeling, our thoughts and feelings have nothing to grab onto and will naturally vanish. The wave returns to the ocean. The clouds vanish in the sky. Thoughts and emotions naturally pass away. As some meditators might know, there is nothing wrong with thoughts and emotions. Only the ego-absorbed thoughts and feelings separate us from the universe of infinite possibilities. Since the ego is filtered by the open heart, when we learn how to think, listen, speak, and act from the heart a new world of wisdom will open its doors to us.

If in the middle of strong emotions and deluded thoughts, we remain present in our hearts, the distinctions between heaven and hell, ordinary and enlightened mind, duality and non-duality will gradually melt away. When we're not trapped in divided consciousness, the dualities of the relative world are not a problem. The interplay of absolute and relative, self and other, extraordinary reality and ordinary reality become a wonderful dance, a luminous play of infinite wisdom.

If we felt connected to everyone else, we wouldn't think of causing them harm. A natural consequence of the Great Heart practice is the awareness that everyone is connected, and that what we do affects everyone else. The heart is our True Self and from it unconditional compassion arises. Devoid of ego, the True Self is unlimited, boundless. It contains everything; and since it contains everything, nothing can defile it.

Soyen Shaku, one of the first Japanese Zen masters to visit the United States last century wrote:

> *Make a searching analysis of yourself. Realize that your body is not your body. It is part of the whole body of sentient beings. Your mind is not your mind. It is but a constituent of all minds. Your*

eyes, your ears, your nose, your tongue, your hands, and your feet
are not merely your individual belongings, but in joint ownership
with all sentient beings. You simply call them yours *and* others.
You cling to your own being and consider others separate from
you. It is nothing but a baseless delusion of yours.[5]

All philosophies, including Buddhist philosophy, are like the finger pointing at the moon. They are not the moon itself. Even if we intellectually accept the notion of True Self, *realizing* it is another matter. In the *Sutras of Forty-Two Sections,* the Buddha said, "If you endeavor to embrace the Way through much learning, the Way will not be understood. If you observe the Way with simplicity of heart, great indeed is the Way."[6] "Simplicity of heart" can only be attained by being present in your heart in each moment, and thus dropping your judgments and projections.

When you can practice from your heart with every fiber of your being, you realize there is no separation between any of us anywhere. Then every moment and every place becomes the enlightened life. Every sound is the sound of enlightenment; every sight is the sight of enlightenment; every place is nirvana. The place where you sit is the land of peace and tranquility—even when you're changing poopy diapers, washing dirty dishes, pulling up weeds, or singing a song.

In one of his writings called *Genjokoan,* Zen Master Dogen describes this enlightened state, where the distinctness of phenomena is not disturbed by their merging into one; and their merging is not hindered by the fact that they are distinct:

> *Gaining enlightenment is like the moon*
> *Reflecting in the water.*
> *The moon does not get wet nor is the water disturbed.*
> *Although its light is extensive and great,*
> *The moon is reflected even in a puddle an inch across.*
> *The whole moon and the whole sky*

Are reflected in a dew drop in the grass,
In one drop of water.
Enlightenment does not disturb the person,
Just as the moon does not disturb the water.
A person does not hinder enlightenment,
Just as a dewdrop does not hinder the moon in the sky.
The depth of the drop is the height of the moon.[7]

At the Zen Center in Los Angeles, Maezumi Roshi gave the following instruction to his students when they entered the meditation hall:

Just be harmonious, like milk dissolved in water. Temporarily, there are the relationships of guests to master and juniors to seniors; however, eventually all of us will be Buddhas forever. We should maintain the heart-mind, moment after moment.

When he says "all of us will be Buddhas forever," Maezumi Roshi is re-affirming that all of us have the capacity to realize our enlightened state. Before realizing our True Self, we grasp onto our ego-self. But looking into that ego-self from the heart, we penetrate its constructs and projections, and as our self-grasping ignorance dissolves, our true source of peace and compassion manifests. The heart-mind is the true source of peace.

NEGATIVE KARMA AND WAR

Through determination and practice, it is possible to transform our negative karma. *Karma* literally means "action" or "deed." According to the laws of karma, as we mentioned in chapter 1, every volitional action leaves an impression or habit that will later act as an unconscious tendency. The actions and reactions in one's life create the imprints for our thoughts, feelings, and subsequent actions. Negative or unwhole-some karma leads to contracted and unhappy states of mind. Positive or wholesome karma leads to expansive, happy states of mind. One does not get punished or rewarded by an outside force; whatever suf-fering there is arises from our unconscious habits. These habits lead to separation from others and from our own heart.

War between countries is a symptom of the alienation and numb-ness of the citizens of the countries at war. The history of the world is composed of the negative and positive thoughts of individuals, not of countries and empires.

The Dalai Lama has written:

> *As a Buddhist I have learned that what principally upsets our in-ner peace is what we call disturbing emotions. All those thoughts, emotions and mental states that reflect a negative or uncompas-sionate state of mind inevitably undermine our experience of in-ner peace...Disturbing emotions are the very source of unethical conduct. They are also the basis of anxiety, depression, confusion and stress.*[8]

We might add that, worst of all, they are the basis of war. Just as global peace depends upon individual peace, war exists due to the bel-licose attitudes and emotions of individuals. It is important that we learn how to filter our disturbing emotions through our hearts to avoid spreading the seeds of war.

We discovered that there are many people who want to help others but they are too scared to open their own hearts. Then they project their own conflicts onto others and act inappropriately. When we learn to feel our own pain wholeheartedly, we can more easily accept and honor the pain of others. Our open heart will guide us to the proper action.

Our greatest obstacle is the delusion in our own minds. With discipline and practice, delusion can transform into loving kindness. Due to a distorted view of reality, we interpret our thoughts and emotions in ways that are completely contrary to the reality of things. One of the largest impediments to creating inner peace is the sickening pleasure we get when we see people we dislike fail. We need to be aware of how we attach pleasure to negativity. Making the effort to not get pleasure out of the misfortunes of others opens up our lives and untwists our karma more than anything else. This way we can release the negative karma that has conditioned our actions and our experience of the world.

In recent years we have been witness to the photos of torture in military prisons that show the pleasure the guards feel from tormenting their captives. This is an extreme case of pleasure attached to negativity. In a smaller measure, we all have experienced it in our own lives. How did you feel when your sibling got punished for an act you did? How about when a fellow employee you dislike gets humiliated by the boss?

It is easy to demonize those we disagree with. It is difficult to embrace them and open the space for transformation. It is difficult to act toward them with compassion when we are not connected to our hearts. When we focus in our hearts, feeling the pain of being punished for what we did, feeling the pain of having someone praised who we dislike, feeling the pain when our favorite team loses the championship, is good pain. It is the pain of our hearts opening up, redirecting our energies and liberating our mindstream. It is wonderful to feel happy when our team wins the championship, but what is twisted is to feel good about the other team losing. Getting pleasure out of other people's misfortunes is a "malignant" pleasure.

Once you catch yourself starting to get pleasure about a negative event, you can redirect your energies by returning your awareness to your heart. The old destructive habit of feeling good about something negative came from the ego, but this attitude cannot survive in the heart. When we are aware of what we are doing, we are already larger than our negative tendency. And thus the negative tendency has space to dissolve.

It takes a lot of effort at the beginning to redirect our energies, so we must always practice returning to our hearts. From the heart we can redirect our energies so we can feel good about positive events and feel the pain of negative events. It is just like breaking a bad habit. It takes a lot of effort when we first try to change it. However, when we no longer get pleasure out of other people's pain and suffering, we realize it was worth all the effort.

PEACE WITHIN, PEACE WITHOUT

Peace in the world starts with each of us realizing peace in our own hearts. When one person realizes peace within, unconditional love naturally flows in the heart. This kind of peace and love is true compassion. This compassion is not a forced attitude. Once we realize inner peace, we will naturally extend peace into our families, our communities, and so on. If we haven't experienced it within ourselves first, we will project our inner fight into the world.

Practicing the heart meditation everyday will allow you to experience a sense of inner peace and emotional wholeness. As you continue to practice this meditation and go deeper within your own heart-mind, your experience of peace and wholeness will increase in intensity. Genuine change can only come from within, allowing us to take full responsibility for our life and thereby make a real contribution to the world.

Consider the story of the aimless young man who came to a Zen master. The young man told him, "I am wasting my life and I want to become your disciple." In order to take him as a disciple, the Zen master made the young man agree to do everything he said. The young man agreed. The master called an elderly monk and set up a *go* board. He told the young man, "You will play *go* with this monk. If you lose, I will cut off your head. If you win, I will cut off the monk's head."

At first the young man was nervous, but later his concentration exceeded anything he had experienced. He was able to place each *go* piece as if it were an extension of his own body and mind. Eventually he had the advantage on the old monk who was also deep in concentration. Then the young man looked into the old monk's eyes and his heart opened up. He told himself, "I have wasted my life and this old man has led a life of devotion and service."

The young man deliberately made a bad move to give the old monk the advantage. At that point the Zen master knocked all of the pieces off the board. He said to the young man, "Now you are ready to be my disciple. First you learned discipline and concentration and then you learned compassion. With awareness and a great heart as the foundation of your practice, you will be able to eliminate all of your bad habits."

There is no freedom without discipline. It does not matter if you are applying discipline toward the understanding of your own mind, toward learning to play a musical instrument or improving your skills in a sport. The great violinist Jascha Heifetz said, "If I don't practice for one day, I know it. If I don't practice for two days, my critics know it. If I don't practice for three days, everyone knows it."[9]

With that kind of discipline, we are able to go beyond the limits of the instrument, the sport, or our own small mind to find peace and freedom. A disciplined mind is essential for happiness and spiritual freedom. That mind encompasses all of your conscious experiences, including your thoughts and feelings. With dedication and effort over time, everyone can definitely accomplish profound transformation in their mental attitudes and consequent actions.

According to Thich Nhat Hanh,[10] the seeds of violence and war are always present in our unconscious mind. In order to prevent them from spreading, we need to maintain awareness of our hearts. By maintaining this, we cultivate the seeds of compassion and understanding and contribute to peace in the world. Since we are all connected, our individual consciousness has an impact on the global consciousness and the global consciousness has an impact on each of us. The ancient Indian sage Vimalakirti said, "As long as one person suffers, I suffer."[11]

Professor William Tiller of Stanford University, a pioneer in psycho-energetic research, said:

> *We are all connected. We are all entangled…there is no real separation between us, so that what we do to another we do to an aspect of ourselves. None of us are innocent in that regard. If there is something out there we don't like; we can't really turn our backs on it because we're co-creators, somehow or another. And we have to do the right things to try to get the future that is best for all of us. That's our responsibility as co-creators.*[12]

We all have done things that are morally reprehensible. We all have character flaws; we all are more or less egocentric, selfish, and petty. And these character flaws have led each of us, many times, to be unloving, spiteful, jealous, and to act in ways that only add to the sum total of distress in the world. But without a doubt, all of us want to contribute to peace in the world and to learn how to resolve conflicts nonviolently.

When we protest unjust acts, we must do it with awareness of the heart's energies of love and compassion—otherwise it becomes another violent act in pursuit of stopping violence. The Buddha said, "Hatred never ceases by hatred, but by love alone is healed."[13] The practice of nonviolence is not just a learned set of techniques or skills. Nonviolence must be our state of being.

ONE BODY, ONE WORLD

If we want to contribute to creating lasting peace in the world, we must be able to maintain awareness in our activities. When we blame others, we are spreading the seeds of war. The seeds of discontent and war are often planted at home. Many children grow up in unhappy homes. Without proper love and education, they often grow into adults who are incapable of loving others, including their own parents. Children can learn to become peaceful from parents who realize peace within.

As the heart illuminates our path, we experience that when we harm others, we harm ourselves; when we benefit others, we benefit ourselves. A sense of responsibility for other beings arises. We naturally want to help them overcome their problems, even if they behave negatively toward us.

If happiness were not dependent on the welfare of others, it would make sense to pursue our own selfish goals. But our lives depend upon the give and take with others. When we look carefully, life is not possible without human interdependence; our own health and well being depends on cooperation and interaction with others.

Before eating our meals at our Zen Center, we chant, "Seventy-two labors brought us this food. We should know how it comes to us." In Zen monasteries, there are traditionally seventy-two positions necessary for the smooth functioning of all activities—including spiritual, liturgical, and administrative, as well as food preparation and manual labor. Without the work of all of these people, the monks would not be able to function or eat. The chant reminds us that our food goes through many hands to arrive at our table, now including the farmers or ranchers, harvesters, transporters, warehouse workers, retailers, cooks, and servers. By lessening the grip of our grasping ego, we begin to see how connected we are and how much our welfare depends on the welfare of others.

Astronaut Rusty Schweickart after his flight on the Apollo 9 wrote,

> *When you go around the earth in an hour and a half, you begin
> to recognize that your identity is with that whole thing. That
> makes a change. You look down and you cannot imagine how
> many borders and boundaries you cross…Hundreds of people
> killing each other over some imaginary line that you are not even
> aware of, you cannot even see it. From where you are, the planet is
> a whole and it is so beautiful and you wish you could take each
> individual by the hand and say: "Look at it from this perspective.
> Look at what is important!"*[14]

True Compassion, Unconditional Love

True compassion is not restricted to those we happen to like. It arises
equally for all beings. Those who act against us test the limits of our patience and realization. Only a mind that is grounded in the heart can
avoid acting with hatred against hatred.

We do not need to kill our negative feelings and emotions in order
to be loving and peaceful. If we try to kill our negative feelings, we
would be creating an internal war. By trying to "kill the enemy of our
delusion," we would only get more entangled in the never-ending
battle of good versus evil. We just need to be aware of our energies
without judging them or acting on them. In this way, our mind is
united with our heart to become the heart-mind.

If someone gets angry with us, we may see that their anger is not
about us at all. Because we can accept our own anger, we can accept
their anger too. And we can see all the pain, frustration, and desperation behind it. Seeing this clearly, we can respond to anger and hatred,
like the Buddha said, with love.

With proper guidance and a heart-mind connection, your personal
life can become your best spiritual teacher. At Great Mountain Zen

Center we have regular Great Heart retreats each year. Most of our students follow the practice described in this book as a complement to their traditional Zen practice.

POWER OF PRAYER

By opening our hearts, we learn how to pray. An open heart is like a spring of compassion that always flows. From this space, a prayer for peace was born. We wrote this prayer after the attack on the World Trade Center on September 11, 2001, and we chant it everyday at the Zen Center:

> *All buddhas, bodhisattvas,*
> *Protectors of the Dharma and the Three Treasures.*
> *With all sentient beings,*
> *I open my heart to transform*
> *Ignorance, violence, and suffering.*
> *May healing and peace prevail*
> *In the Dharma Worlds.*
> *Maha Prajna Paramita.*

First we invoke the presence of all the enlightened beings and guardians to be present and hear our prayer. The Three Treasures represent the unity and diversity of creations and their harmonious relationships. The "Dharma Worlds" means everywhere we can imagine and cannot imagine. The Dharma is all phenomena. The final line literally means "the great wisdom that carries us from the shore of delusion to the shore of enlightenment." It is Buddhist way of saying *Amen.*

A *bodhisattva* is an enlightened being who dedicates his or her life to liberating all beings everywhere. The Christian equivalent would be an angel. In many branches of Buddhism, the congregation recites four Bodhisattva vows. Here is our version, which we recite daily with an open heart and an attitude of prayer:

> *Creations are numberless,*
> *I vow to receive them.*
> *Delusions are inexhaustible,*
> *I vow to dissolve them.*
> *Dharma Gates are omnipresent,*
> *I vow to experience them.*
> *The Enlightened Way is unsurpassable,*
> *I vow to manifest it.*

May each of you realize the power of your own heart and may that power become a beacon for peace in the world.

APPENDIX

SUMMARY: EIGHT STEPS
ON THE GREAT HEART WAY

If you want to open your heart and contribute to peace in the world, we encourage you to initiate a daily practice of awareness based on the Great Heart Way. The first seven steps of this method are simple and straightforward, but they do require determination, courage, whole-heartedness, and patience. The eighth step is your lifelong practice. We invite you to begin on the road to emotional wholeness and spiritual harmony by learning this brief summary of the Great Heart Way:

1. Use the concentration developed in your meditation to be aware of recurring uncomfortable feelings and situations.

2. Connect with your heart and feel the emotions that manifest in each situation. Without getting lost in discursive thoughts or judgments, simply *feel* whatever arises.

3. When you feel your emotions thoroughly, an associated un-conscious fixed image will eventually appear.

4. To find the belief or wrong conclusion that supports this image, ask yourself what you said to yourself at the time when the image formed.

5. To deprogram the image, visualize yourself at the time of the event. Give emotional, mental, and physical support to yourself as a child—all the support that you needed but didn't get.

6. Notice how your positive and negative energies get crossed. For instance, notice when you feel good about negative events. Make an effort to untangle these crossed energies. Feeling good must respond to positive events and feeling bad must respond to negative events. In this way, your energies will reunify into one mindstream.

7. Do this again. And do it again. Keep doing it.

8. Learn to breathe through your heart and continue connecting with your heart in your daily life.

If we follow these steps over and over again, by the mere fact that we are repeating them, this process will become simple, familiar, natural, and spontaneous.

Appendix

EXERCISES

EXERCISES FROM CHAPTER 3

Sit in meditation for at least twenty minutes daily. If you have to skip a day, that's okay, but return to your daily schedule of meditation as soon as you can. When you finish your meditation, spend some time answering the questions below. You don't have to remain in meditation posture; you can sit at a table to write your answers. Depending on your time, do one or more. Record your answers in your journal.

These questions will help you identify your hidden beliefs. If any of them bring up a strong emotional response, connect with your heart and take time to feel the physical sensation of that emotion. Breathe deeply. Let go of the storyline and return your focus to the physical sensation. And continue to breathe deeply. Your responses to the exercises are neither good nor bad. They just are. For now, remember to maintain a nonjudgmental attitude when you answer the questions. This means to accept the answers without judging whether they are right or wrong, taking them with the same accepting attitude that compassionate parents have for their infant. They accept the infant whether she or he is calm or crying. In the same way, we recommend that you accept your answers—whatever they are—without judging them.

Meditation is the foundation of the Great Heart Way. Following the instructions in this book on how to meditate, and doing so regularly, are the keys to effectively put this method into practice. Learning how to focus the mind is of great importance, because when we learn to meditate we begin to experience some detachment from our thoughts and feelings. This detachment helps us to work with the following exercises to effectively bring the Great Heart Way into our lives. It signals we are starting to experience that we are actually more than our thoughts and feelings, that we are a large container in which thoughts and feelings can arise and dissolve.

As we mentioned in the introduction, we recommend that you read this book (while you are developing your meditation practice) at least once before you attempt to do the exercises. There is a lot of information throughout the book that will teach you how to work with the feelings and thoughts that may arise when doing these exercises. The exercises may create strong feelings in you, but these feelings are great opportunities to practice the Great Heart Way.

To provide a bit of summary instruction:

If uncomfortable feelings arise, do not try to overpower them. Just breathe. Connect with your heart and feel the pain underlying the discomfort. Let go of the storyline about the feelings. Then ask yourself, "Where does the pain come from?" In this way, the answer will be sprouting from the actual pain that is emanating from somewhere in your body. It won't be just an abstraction or fictitious story that you create in your head in order to avoid feeling the sensation in depth. It is very different to have the answer spring into your consciousness from your body than it is to have it come from your head. You will feel the answer with your whole body as a release of energy. Then set that answer aside and keep feeling whatever sensations arise. The same procedure will apply if any of the following questions make you feel very

angry. Take a deep breath. Connect with your heart and allow yourself
to feel the anger. Where is it in your body? Do not try to justify the
anger, but instead feel the pain underlying it. What is this pain about?
Let go of any answers that appear and just keep feeling. If you can follow these steps you are already practicing the Great Heart Way. Always
record your answers in your journal.

You do not need to work with these exercises within any particular time frame. You can take as much or as little time as you want. We
recommend you approach the exercises after you have practiced meditation, because your mind will be more open and spontaneous. At
that time you can decide how many questions you want to answer.

If nothing comes to mind regarding a particular question, that's
okay. Just skip it for now. You can always try again later. Something
might arise for you when you least expect it.

During meditation you should focus your mind on your breathing,
not these exercises. But if when working with them you feel the need
to sit in meditation again to think quietly about an exercise or to
connect with your heart and feel your emotions, we encourage you
to do that.

1. Situations that reoccur in our lives may seem random or co-
   incidental. Looking more deeply, we may find these events
   occur as the result of hidden images and beliefs formed early
   in life. To transform these, we must first become aware of
   them. Settling the mind in meditation makes it possible to
   concentrate on these subtle issues. After sitting in meditation,
   write your answers to the following questions:

      a. Are there reoccurring patterns of feelings or situations
         in your life that appear to be random and uncon-
         nected to anything in particular?

b. What situations make you angry?

c. What situations make you sad?

d. Do you feel like a victim of circumstances? When?

e. What kind of people do you hate?

f. What kind of people do you love?

g. Do you get in trouble at work or school? What happens when you do?

h. How do you feel when you meet new people?

These questions will give you clues to what is relevant or important for you.

2. Reflecting on these seemingly random patterns or situations, what emotions do you associate with them? Write down how you feel when these incidents occur.

Connect with your heart and just feel. Do not identify with any thoughts that might arise about these feelings. Do not listen to any stories fabricated in your head about them. If there are stories in your mind, don't fight them. Just return your attention to the sensations and feel them with your whole body. Record your experiences in your journal.

Exercises from chapter 4

The following exercises offer ways to find clues to your hidden images. The best clues are found in the repetitive patterns of discomfort in your life. When discomfort and emotional pain arise, connect with your heart and stay with the pain. Don't look for your hidden images. They will be uncovered by bringing awareness to your feelings, and by staying with them without judgments or stories.

Before doing the following exercises, it is again recommended that you meditate for at least twenty minutes. Then carefully read the exercises and reflect on them throughout the day. Always maintain your heart-mind connection and keep writing your responses to the questions in your journal.

1. Do you remember your early hateful feelings, including hateful feelings towards yourself?

2. What are your early memories of feeling guilt?

3. Do you remember childhood thoughts of not being loved enough and/or feeling that others were loved more than you? What conclusions did you draw about not being loved enough?

4. Can you recall any behavioral strategies that developed to compensate for what you perceived as a lack of love?

5. What standards do you set for yourself to make up for what you perceived as your faults?

6. Which one of the three deluded attitudes—submission, aggression, or withdrawal—did you primarily adopt?

    a. How do traces of the other attitudes manifest in your life?

    b. How do you use each of these attitudes? What role do they play in your life?

    c. What are you hiding behind these attitudes?

    d. How would you approach your life without depending on deluded attitudes?

7. Ask your closest friend what she or he considers to be your virtues and faults. Put these in two columns: virtues and faults. Watch your reactions, but do not try to change them and do not identify with them. Record how you felt when you received this feedback.

EXERCISES FROM CHAPTER 5

As always, precede the exercises with at least twenty minutes of sitting meditation practice. Increase this to thirty minutes, if you can. Then reflect on the exercises that follow. If you don't have much time, just do one exercise a day. Record your response in your journal right away; or, reflect on the exercise until the end of the day and record your response then. Be sure to always maintain your heart-mind connection.

We recommend working with your images while sitting in the meditation posture. This posture is particularly helpful because it supports the mind as it concentrates on hidden issues while meditating. You can focus your attention on any images that might have arisen, and ask yourself what conclusion you drew at the time.

1. Look at your behavior patterns, as a child and as an adult. For example, as a child, did you hide your true feelings for fear others would reject you? Did you agree to do things just to please others, even when you strongly didn't want to? Did you try to dominate others to avoid facing your vulnerability?

   a. What patterns do you find?
   b. Can you recall the beliefs that underlie these patterns?

    c In the present, are you overly assertive or overly passive?

    d. Do you act aloof and superior, as a way to protect yourself?

    e. What makes you uncontrollably angry? What do you most hate?

Write down your observations. Try not to judge yourself. There is nothing "bad" about anything you discover. You are simply learning about things that you've hidden from yourself.

2. Be aware of repetitive and familiar thoughts, feelings, and re-actions that cause you discomfort or pain. When you find them, ask yourself, "When did I first experience this?" "In what circumstances did this arise in my life?" Feel all the emotions in your body. If you have a moment, sit in medita-tion and continue to experience your emotions. You do not have to count or focus on the breaths now. Your concentra-tion should be connecting with your heart while you feel your feelings. No matter what arises, allow the feelings to be, without identifying with any thoughts you might have about them. Record your experience.

3. What memories arise, after feeling your emotions thoroughly? If a vivid, old memory appears, this is the image. There might be many layers of unfelt feelings. If you've been emotionally numb for a long period of time, it may take longer to find an image. That's okay! Just feel what you feel, without any expec-tations. By doing this work over and over, your body will be-come sensitive again. Eventually, without pressure, an image will surface in your conscious mind.

4. When an image appears, find the emotional belief and wrong conclusion that arose from it. To do this, ask yourself, "What did I tell myself at the time of this event?" Then write down the exact words you said. If you cannot recall the exact words, just keep trying by asking yourself the same questions until these words manifest to you. The fixed image is trapped within a statement you made a long time ago about your reality and the world around you. In order to liberate the image, you must bring that statement into your conscious mind.

5. Heal the image by visualizing yourself at the time of the event. Close your eyes, sit erect on your meditation cushion or chair. Visualize giving all the emotional, mental, and physical support to yourself as a child that you had needed, but didn't get.

Remember: No matter how long it takes, an image will appear. For some it may take longer than for others, but throughout the process you will be getting in touch with your emotions and feeling more alive. It is well-invested time and effort.

Exercises from chapter 6

Preceding these exercises, do your twenty minutes of meditation. If possible, increase the time you spend meditating. Sitting in meditation mornings and evenings will help improve awareness. Even if you can't do this every day, consider doing it sometimes. Then reflect on the exercises and write your responses in your journal.

Some of these exercises require reflection throughout the day. So read them, answer what you can in your journal, and then think about them as you continue through the day. At the end of the day or maybe the next day, write some more in response to these questions. Always remember to maintain your heart-mind connection.

1. What feelings, attitudes, and beliefs prevent you from being satisfied with your life now?

   a. When you are dissatisfied or unhappy, experience the feelings that arise.
   b. Is there a pattern?

2. What do you want to be different in your life?

   a. What feelings, attitudes, and beliefs prevent you from changing?
   b. What is the fear that prevents you from shifting your beliefs?

3. Be aware of destructive *thoughts*. Don't try to shut them down. Just be aware without interfering with them.

   a. Write down significant thoughts that you would ordinarily shut down, but can now allow to be there.

4. Be aware of disturbing *emotions*. Do not try to shut them off. Just feel your emotions without trying to interpret them.

   a. Write down significant emotions that you would ordinarily shut down but now allow yourself to feel.

5. Note when you find yourself feeling good about negative feelings or thoughts, and write it down. Allow yourself to feel the pleasure attached to the destructiveness. You must be very aware of this. Then you can allow your mindstream to reconvert itself.

    a. What are the consequences when, for the sake of momentary satisfaction, you give in to destructive impulses?

    b. What choices do you make as you observe the destructive attitudes and intentions within you?

    c. Record the times when you cross your positive and negative energies.

    d. In what ways does this destructiveness manifest? How does it affect your life?

6. When do you notice your positive mindstream responding to positive events?

7. When do you notice your negative mindstream responding to negative events?

ACKNOWLEDGMENTS

We especially want to acknowledge our parents, Ilia and Julio and Samuel and Lylyan, and children, Lucas and Roldan and Sam, David and Dan and Lily, for helping to cultivate the karmic seeds that grew into this work. We give special recognition to our siblings, Tito, Maricusa, Masaro and Izaskun and Alan, Barry, and Barbara for sharing our childhoods together. Without our teachers, Philip Kapleau Roshi, Pat Hawk Roshi, Taizan Maezumi Roshi, Bernie Glassman Roshi, and Sochu Suzuki Roshi, the Lotus Flower would not have grown.

The unconditional trust, love, and support of our students provided the fertilizer that nourished the seeds. We especially want to thank Paul Gyodo Agostinelli, Richard Shinzen Blackmore, Kent Brown, Nick Coffey, Heather Kuden Collins, Suzanne Kyokan DeAtley, Carlos Gento Estrella, Michael Gump, Ed Gensha Hansen, Michael Jensen, John Izzo Isaacs, Barbara Kammer, Christopher Melton, Laura Minks, Geoff O'Keefe, Adam Richardson, Jill Riley, John Fugetsu Rueppel, John Schoonbrood, Andrew Hakuju Smith, Kevin Muryo Tennant, Yvonne Genan Timmers, Rich Goho Torres, and David Kyokei Young.

We appreciate the encouragement of our friends and fellow travelers: Dennis Genpo Merzel Roshi, Nicolee Jikyo McMahon Roshi, Wendy Egyoku Nakao Roshi, Pat Enkyo O'Hara Roshi, Joan Halifax Roshi, Anne Seisen Saunders Sensei, Paul Genki Kahn, Padma Wick, Sean Murphy, Julie Robbins, Judith Putnam, Ed and Kathy Wydallis, Josh White, Paul Jeffrey, Deborah Bowman, and Ramon Melcon.

We acknowledge with gratitude a grant from the Frederick P. Lenz Foundation for American Buddhism (www.fredericklenzfoundation.org) whose support was vital to the completion of this work.

We also thank our editors at Wisdom Publications for understanding our vision and for giving us the encouragement and support we needed to complete this book, and for precise and skillful editing that smoothed many rough passages and helped clarify our presentation.

Ilia Shinko Perez
Gerry Shishin Wick
Great Mountain Zen Center
Lafayette, Colorado
May 2006
www.gmzc.org

NOTES

INTRODUCTION

1   This quote of John Pierrakos, M.D., founder of Bioenergetics, comes from his book *Core Energetics.*

2   See William James, *Varieties of Religious Experience.*

3   This quote appears on page 5 of Eugene Gendlin's book, *Focusing.*

4   See page 54 in the book *The Three Pillars of Zen,* edited by Philip Kapleau.

5   See epigram in chapter 1 and footnote 1, chapter 1 and Alexander Lowen who wrote in *Joy,* p. 12, "[feelings] are the life of the body."

CHAPTER 1

1   The author and philosopher Aldous Huxley extensively explor the nature of the unconscious. The quote comes from *The Perennial Philosophy.*

2   The "Infinite Mind" or "Absolute" is beyond all language. As soon as it is described, those words are inadequate. Some new words, such as "is-ness" "this-ness," "such-ness," and "thus-ness" have been invented to point to the nature of the Absolute. In the ninth century when Chinese Zen Master Ganto Zenkatsu was asked about the Absolute,

he said "It is *just this.*" See *The Book of Equanimity,* case 50. It adds nothing extra and it does not exclude anything. Since it is beyond all concepts, it transcends space and time, ego, self, and other. In the twelfth century, Chinese Zen Master Mumon Ekai versified this Infinite Mind or True Self in case 47 of his *Mumonkan* (The Gateless Gate) (See *Zen Comments on the Mumonkan*):

> *This one instant, as it is, is an infinite number of eons.*
> *An infinite number of eons is at the same time this one instant.*
> *If you see into this fact,*
> *The True Self which is seeing has been seen into.*

3   For the reference to this quote, see footnote 1, chapter 2.

4   See Fred Alan Wolf's *Mind into Matter: A New Alchemy of Science and Spirit.*

5   Candace Pert, *Molecules of Emotion: The Science Behind Mind-Body Medicine.*

6   The famous Japanese Zen Master Dogen was a prolific writer in the thirteenth century. Although Dogen was critical of many of his contemporaries and predecessors, he heaped praise on Gensha Shibi, a tenth-century Zen master, in the chapter *Ikkamyoju* (One Bright Pearl) from Dogen's masterpiece, *Shobogenzo* (The Eye and Treasury of the True Law). Gensha is quoted as saying, "The entire universe is one bright pearl. When you understand, then even in the Black Mountain Cave of Demons complete freedom is functioning."

7   Robert Bly used the analogy of a movie projector for the shadow in his book *A Little Book on the Human Shadow.*

8   The verse is found in case 30 of the collection of Zen koans, *Mumonkan* (Gateless Gate). They can be found in *Zen Comments on the Mumonkan* by Zenkei Shibayama.

9   See Stanislav Grof, *Psychology of the Future,* p. 300.

10 The parable of the "Gem in the Jacket" appears in chapter 8 of the Lotus Sutra, which is one of the most influential and popular texts expounding the teachings of the Buddha. It was written in India approximately 2,300 years ago.

11 The Great Heart Way mainly focuses on the postnatal experiences of the individual or personal unconscious. Some prominent researchers have recognized other layers of the unconscious. In his book *The*

Archetypes and the Collective Unconscious, Jung wrote "…his personal unconscious rests upon a deeper layer which does not derive from personal experience and is not a personal acquisition but is inborn. This deeper layer I call the collective unconscious. I have chosen the term 'collective' because this part of the unconscious is not individual but universal."While the personal unconscious contains contents which were at one time conscious but which have disappeared from our awareness through repression or loss of memory, the contents of the collective unconscious were never acquired individually but owe their existence to heredity and human nature.

Through many years of investigation, Grof demonstrated that prenatal experiences are an important part of the individual unconscious. (See *Psychology of the Future*.) It is possible to access prenatal experiences and the collective unconscious using the methods described in this book. However, we will further investigate these realms in our future work. The Great Heart method is similar to peeling the layers of an onion. The deeper you go, the more subtle realms of your unconscious are revealed.

12 This famous quote of Supreme Court Justice Potter Stewart was part of his brief on the case Jacobellis vs. Ohio in 1964. The case involved the showing of the French motion picture *Les Amants* (The Lovers), which the state had deemed obscene. Justice Stewart concluded with the majority of the court, "I know [pornography] when I see it, and the motion picture involved in this case is not that." (See U.S. Supreme Court case *Jacobellis v. Ohio,* 378 U.S. 184 [1964].)

13 Psychologist and Buddhist practitioner John Welwood used the phrase "spiritual bypassing" in his book *Toward a Psychology of Awakening.*

14 There are many examples of famous scientists who did not use conceptual thinking to solve important scientific problems. One form of non-conceptual thinking is visualization, which is used in Tibetan Buddhist meditation. In his autobiography (see *Albert Einstein: Philosopher-Scientist*), Einstein wrote that his theory of special relativity originated when he visualized himself riding on a light beam. Colleagues of Nobel laureate I. I. Rabi said that Rabi could visualize riding on an electron.

The dream state is also responsible for many important discoveries. Chemist August Kekule discovered the structure of benzene, one of the most important structures in organic chemistry, through a dream. The structure is in the form of a ring, a circle of six carbon atoms. This organic structure had puzzled scientists for a long time. Kekule wrote, "The atoms were gamboling before my eyes; all twining and twisting in snakelike motion. But look! What was that? One of the snakes had seized hold of its own tail, and the form whirled mockingly before my eyes. As if by a flash of lighting I awoke" (quoted by Arthur Koestler in *The Act of Creation*). The Nobel laureate Niels Bohr also made his most important physics discoveries in dreams.

In his autobiography, Nobel laureate Luis Alvarez wrote how his father told him to "just sit and think" whenever he was stumped by a problem. Alvarez discovered many important principles in physics during his "contemplative meditation." In contrast, near the end of his creative life, Nobel laureate Wolfgang Pauli complained, "Ach! I know too much!" (quoted by laureate Leon Lederman in an interview; see http://www.achievement.org/autodoc/ page/led0int-8). He was not able to quiet his mind and open it to new paradigms.

15 I (Shishin) first heard Professor John Isaacs of the Scripps Institution of Oceanography mention "the tyranny of the first successful solution" when we were asked by the U.S. Navy to help develop methods to keep undersea divers warm when they dived to deep depths. The Navy's "Hot Wet Suit" program was looking for solutions to keep the water around the diver's body warm. Professor Isaacs and I showed that divers lost most of their heat through their lungs, not through their skin. We presented a solution that kept the divers warm by moisturizing and heating the air that they breathed. But the Navy rejected it since it did not involve a "hot wet suit."

16 Japanese Zen Master Dogen wrote these famous lines in his *Genjo Koan* (The Way of Everyday Life). The next two lines continue: "To study the self is to forget the self. To forget the self is to be enlightened by all things." Dogen is telling us that when we let go of our ego-grasping

mind, our entire life is the enlightened life. We have used the translation by Taizan Maezumi found in *The Way of Everyday Life*.

17 German physicist Werner Heisenberg won the Nobel Prize in 1932 for his contributions to quantum physics that include his "Heisenberg Uncertainty Principle." Although initially this principle states that a measurement of the position of a particle disturbs its momentum, in popular culture it came to be explained that the observation of an event changes the event.

18 See *The Little Prince*.

19 When I (Shishin) was training at the Zen Center of Los Angeles, I received a glowing testament to the healing power of unconditional presence. A well-known psychiatrist who was on the faculty at UCLA and who had a thriving private practice in Westwood, told me, "The more I practice meditation, the less I have to say to my patients and the better they get."

CHAPTER 2

1 Although Jung did not seem to have a meditation practice himself, he saw the value of meditation and recognized that it has the potential to access the unconscious. This quote appears in the *Collected Works of C. G. Jung: vol. II, Psychology and Religion: East and West,* second edition, page 508. And the entire quote says, "The meditation our text *[The Tibetan Book of the Great Liberation]* has in mind seems to be a sort of Royal Road to the unconscious."

2 The story of Mr. Sei and his horse is attributed to the Chinese Taoist sage, Lieh Tzu, who lived 2,500 years ago. It was published in 1977 in *Tao: The Watercourse Way,* the last book written by Alan Watts who popularized Eastern religions in the West, particularly Zen and Taoism.

3 Zen Master Bankei Kyosai lived in the seventeenth century and was highly revered in his native Japan. His teachings have been translated into English in *Bankei Zen* by Peter Haskel. This quote comes from one of his sermons.

4   Albert Einstein wrote extensively about the nature of scientific dis-
    covery and about his own creative processes. See *Ideas and Opinions* by
    Einstein and his autobiography in *Albert Einstein: Philosopher-Scientist,*
    edited by P. A. Schlipp.

5   These quotes about seeing the truth were written in the sixth century
    by Kanchi Sosan, the Third Ancestor of Zen in China. His famous
    verse, "Affirming Faith in Mind," is about how to attain enlighten-
    ment, and it remains as relevant and accessible today as it was 1,500
    years ago. For a modern commentary on his teachings, see Dennis
    Genpo Merzel, *The Eye Never Sleeps.*

6   See *Psychology of the Future* by Stanislav Grof.

7   This quote comes from Erwin Schrödinger, *Mind and Matter.* Also see
    Ken Wilber's *Quantum Questions.*

8   Referring to the difficulties and pain that a true seeker must endure
    in order to realize enlightenment, Zen Master Dogen used this
    analogy of the plum blossom. It can be found in *Dogen's Extensive
    Record* translated by Taigen Dan Leighton and Shohokau Okumura,
    discourse 34 on p. 103.

9   See footnote 16, chapter 1.

10 See footnote 5, chapter 2.

CHAPTER 3

1   This quote from Rainer Maria Rilke comes from his work *Letters to a
    Young Poet.*

2   See footnote 1, chapter 1.

3   Alexander Lowen, M.D., was the founder of Bioenergetics and is
    quoted from his book *Bioenergetics,* p. 44.

4   John Welwood, *Toward a Psychology of Awakening,* p. 165.

5   The complete quote of Meister Eckhart is as follows:

> A human being has so many skins inside, covering the depths
> of the heart. We know so many things, but we don't know
> ourselves! Why, thirty or forty skins or hides, as thick and hard
> as an ox's or bear's, cover the soul. Go into your own ground
> and learn to know yourself there.

6 In his book *Thoughts Without a Thinker,* on psychoanalysis from a
   Buddhist perspective, psychiatrist Mark Epstein wrote:

   At the first cross-cultural meetings of Eastern masters and
   Western therapists, the Dalai Lama was incredulous at the notion of "low self-esteem" that he kept hearing about. He went
   around the room asking each Westerner there, "Do you have
   this? Do you have this?" When they all nodded yes, he just
   shook his head in disbelief. (p. 177)

7 According to the National Institute of Mental Health (www.nimh.
   nih.gov/publicat/invisible.cfm), serious depression in the United
   States affects 12 percent of women and 7 percent of men each year. In
   a larger frame, nearly everyone will at some time in their life be af-
   fected by depression—their own or someone else's, clinical or sub-
   clinical. A study by the World Health Organization (Murray CJL and
   Lopez AD, editors, "Summary: The global burden of disease: a com-
   prehensive assessment of mortality and disability from diseases, in-
   juries, and risk factors in 1990 and projected to 2020," [Cambridge,
   Mass.: Published by the Harvard School of Public Health on behalf of
   the World Health Organization and the World Bank, Harvard University Press, 1996]) predicts that depression will be second only to heart
   disease as the major cause of death by the year 2020.

8 There are a number of scientists today who are concluding that mind
   and body are one inseparable reality. Larry Dossey, M.D., of the National Institute of Health, has written extensively on the healing
   power of prayer. See *Healing Words.*
       In controlled experiments with rats in the 1970s, Professor
   Robert Ader of the University of Rochester showed that the mind
   can affect the immune system. There is also the well-known story of
   author Norman Cousins, who cured himself of a life-threatening disease by watching old comedic movies and belly-laughing regularly.
   He chronicled his recovery in the best-selling *Anatomy of an Illness as
   Perceived by the Patient: Reflections on Healing and Regeneration.*

9 Sri Ramakrishna is a nineteenth-century Hindu guru. His teachings
   have been recorded by his disciples in *The Gospel of Sri Ramakrishna.*

10 This quote from Jesus will not be found in chapter and verse of the
   New Testament, but is from Saint Thomas in the Gnostic gospels
   found in the Nag Hammadi dig. See Elaine Pagels, *Beyond Belief: The
   Secret Gospel of Thomas.*

11 Since karma originated in the theologies and cosmologies of Hin-
   duism and Buddhism, for further information about karma, it would
   be best to read authors with backgrounds in those religions. We recommend *What the Buddha Taught* by Walpola Rahula.

12 C. G. Jung wrote extensively about the nature of the unconscious
   mind and the shadow. We particularly recommend *The Undiscovered
   Self* and *Memories, Dreams, Reflections.*

13 Alexander Lowen, M.D., was the founder of Bioenergetics and is
   quoted from page 11 of his book, *Joy.*

14 See pages 42–43 of Alexander Lowen's *Bioenergetics.*

15 This story is included in Paul Reps' book *Zen Flesh, Zen Bones,* which
   contains a number of other famous Zen stories.

16 The Bengali writer and poet Rabindranath Tagore introduced his religious poetry to the West in his volume *Gutanjali,* where he wrote
   about joy from his insight as a Hindu. He received the Nobel Prize
   for literature in 1913.

17 See "Matters of the Heart" by Dr. Gabor Maté on the Web at
   www.shared-vision.com/2005/sv1802/mattersofheart1802.html.

18 See Alexander Lowen's book, *Joy.*

19 This quote of Zen Master Dogen comes from "Hotsu Mujo Shin"
   (Arising the Supreme Thought). You can read the whole essay and
   other excellent translations of Dogen in *How to Raise an Ox* by Francis Dojun Cook.

CHAPTER 4

1 Hermann Hesse won the Nobel Prize for literature in 1946. This
   quote is from one of his later works, *Damien,* influenced by his experience with psychoanalysis and his search for spiritual fulfillment.

2   Milarepa, who lived in the eleventh and twelfth centuries, is one of the greatest saints of Tibetan Buddhism. This quote comes from his spiritual songs, which are tremendous sources of inspiration in Tibetan Buddhism. See *The Hundred Thousand Songs of Milarepa*.

3   Stanislav Grof traces the first conditioning in life to prenatal experiences. The Great Heart Way mostly addresses postnatal experiences, although it does not exclude prenatal conditioning. Once one frees the mind of postnatal conditioning, one might start to experience the underlying layers of conditioning which arose in the womb and from the trauma of birth. See *Psychology of the Future*.

4   In Latin, *ego* literally means "I." For the purposes of this book, we view the ego as what most people consider to be who they are, particularly as distinguished from others. The Buddha taught that the ego is an illusion, and all of our self-images and projections are concepts that have no substantial existence. Psychoanalysis, a source of much thought on the ego, approaches it in a somewhat different manner.

5   See footnote 5, chapter 2.

6   Japanese Zen Master Hakuin wrote his wonderful verse "Song of Zazen" or "Chant in Praise of Zazen" in the eighteenth century. See Philip Kapleau, *Zen Dawn in the West*, p. 181.

7   We adapted our list from pages 93–117 of *Emotional Alchemy* by Tara Bennett-Goleman, where she presented Dr. Jeffrey Young's model of maladaptive schemas.

8   Distorted attitudes can be described in an infinite number of ways. For our purposes, we use the simple and straightforward division of submission, aggression, and withdrawal as articulated by Eva Pierrakos in her book *Fear No Evil*. Her husband, John Pierrakos, a colleague of Wilhelm Reich and co-founder of the Bioenergetic Therapy, divided patterns of denial into five character types in his book *Core Energetics*. They are as follows: *oral* (demands from others and blames them if not satisfied), *masochistic* (feels victimized and builds walls from others), *schizoid* (does not know boundaries and is disoriented and unstable), *aggressive* (tries to control and manipulate others), and *rigid* (not open to others and lacks intimacy). There are even more complex models of denial-based dysfunction.

9 Chinese Zen Master Ummon lived in the ninth and tenth centuries and was considered one of the most brilliant masters during the Golden Age of Zen. This quote comes from case 6 of *The Blue Cliff Record*, a collection of Zen koans. See *Secrets of the Blue Cliff Record* translated by Thomas Cleary.

10 Torei Zenji was an eighteenth-century Zen master who wrote "Bodhisattva Vow." See Robert Aitken, *Encouraging Words*, p. 176.

11 See Tenko Nishida, *A New Road to Ancient Truth*, p. 183.

Chapter 5

1 The quote from Rainer Maria Rilke comes from his first collection of poems, *The Book of Hours: Love Poems to God*.

2 See page 5 of Alexander Lowen's book, *Joy*.

3 "The Identity of Relative and Absolute" is a Zen chant or sutra. You can find a commentary on it in Bernie Glassman's book, *Infinite Circle*.

4 See Tara Bennett-Goleman, *Emotional Alchemy*, p. 228.

5 See Jack Kornfield, *A Path with Heart*, pp. 115–16.

Chapter 6

1 This quote of Jung comes from *Aion*, based on his later research into the phenomenology of the self.

2 D. T. Suzuki was the most prolific translator and popularizer of Zen Buddhism for English readers in the twentieth century. See *On Mahayana Buddhism*, edited by E. Conze.

3 See footnote 7, chapter 2.

4 Bernie Glassman is the founder of the Zen Peacemaker Order, which is dedicated to personal and societal transformation through their three tenets: not knowing, bearing witness to joy and suffering, and healing ourselves and others. Their practice includes street retreats with the homeless and retreats at places of persecution, such as Auschwitz. See *Bearing Witness*.

5 See *Psychology of the Future* by Stanislav Grof.

6   Misunderstandings of the relationship between good and evil as as-
    pects of one reality have had a strong impact on the history of human-
    ity. Elaine Pagels, professor of religion at Princeton University, was
    researching the "myth of Satan" for her book *The Origin of Satan,* and
    learned "When people said things like 'Satan is trying to take over this
    country,' they didn't mean some kind of vague supernatural energy
    out there. They meant certain people who were motivated by the
    forces of evil and they could give you names and addresses. The
    mythology of Satan clearly has a much deeper resonance [in the un-
    consciousness of people] than I, and many like me, had thought"
    (from an interview in *Tricycle: The Buddhist Review,* Summer 2005).
    When this belief translates into political behavior, there clearly is no
    room for negotiating. In *Memories, Dreams, Reflections,* Jung wrote,
    "The individual who wishes to have an answer to the problem of evil,
    as it is posed today, has need, first and foremost, of self-knowledge;
    that is, the utmost possible knowledge of his own wholeness." In
    Matthew 5:39, Jesus told his disciples, "Do not resist evil." Only when
    one accepts his evil tendencies can the evil be transformed. When one
    resists evil, then it becomes an enemy, as opposed to something that
    can be integrated into a whole person and used for creative, positive
    purposes.

7   Thanks to Cindy Smock for sharing the Jungian interpretation of
    "Sleeping Beauty."

8   This quote from Rainer Maria Rilke comes from his work *Letters to a
    Young Poet.*

9   Rumi was a thirteenth-century Persian mystic and poet. His works
    are highly regarded in Sufism, the mystical movement within Islam.
    After Rumi's death, his disciples formed an order that is known in the
    West as the whirling dervishes. This quote comes from his major work
    Masnavi-ye Manavi in *Teachings of Rumi (The Masnavi): The Spiritual
    Couplets of Jalaludin Rumi.*

10 See *Wild Ivy: The Spiritual Autobiography of Zen Master Hakuin,* trans-
    lated by Norman Wadell.

11 This quote comes from the fictionalized account of the life of the Buddha written by Hermann Hesse in *Siddhartha*.

12 This Taoist quote comes from the book *Huainanzi* produced through the patronage of Liu An, King of Huainin, and his followers in China in the second century B.C.E.

13 See Aristotle, *The Nicomachean Ethics.*

Chapter 7

1   See Alexander Lowen's *Bioenergetics*, p. 44.

2   This widely quoted saying of Pope John Paul II (1920–2005) came from one of his speeches.

3   Pema Chodron is an American nun in the Tibetan Buddhist tradition. She is a disciple of the late Chögyam Trungpa Rinpoche, who founded a number of Tibetan Buddhist training centers in the West, as well as the Buddhist-oriented Naropa University in Boulder, Colorado. Pema Chodron has written a number of popular books, including *The Places That Scare You: A Guide to Fearlessness in Difficult Times.*

4   From the article by Stephen Harrod Buhner in *Spirituality and Health,* April 2006.

5   Soyen Shaku was the first Zen master to come to America. He attended the World Parliament of Religions in Chicago in 1893, and then returned in 1905 to teach for a year. Two of his students, D. T. Suzuki and Nyogen Senzaki, had a profound effect on the establishment of Zen in America. Shaku's "The First Step in Zazen," which contains this quote, appears in *Like a Dream, Like a Fantasy,* edited by Eido Shimano.

6   Soyen Shaku wrote about the "Sutra of 42 Sections" in *Sermons of a Buddhist Abbot: A Classic of American Buddhism* and in his book *Zen for Americans.*

7   This passage comes from "Genjokoan," which is one of the most widely read and famous verses by Zen Master Dogen. We use the translation by Taizan Maezumi found in *The Way of Everyday Life.*

8   This quote of the Dalai Lama comes from his foreword to the book by Tara Bennett-Goleman, *Emotional Alchemy.*

9 This quote about practicing has been attributed to a wide range of musicians, including greats such as Yehudi Menuhin, Jan Pederewski, Arthur Rubenstein, composer Franz Liszt, and popular conductor Doc Severnson. Since the most references are to Jascha Heifetz as the author, we included his name in the main text.

10 Thich Nhat Hanh is a Vietnamese Buddhist monk and peace activist. He has written more than one hundred books in which he strives to promote his vision of nonviolent civil disobedience and to translate the teachings of the Buddha into language that everyone can understand. His quotes are taken from the book *Creating True Peace*.

11 The Vimalakirti Sutra is highly esteemed in Chinese and Japanese Buddhism. It contains the teachings of a lay adherent of the Buddha who debates with some of the Buddha's disciples about the nature of reality. Due to his experience of the interconnectedness of all beings, Vimalakirti was able to say, "As long as one person suffers, I suffer." See *The Vimalakirti Nirdesa Sutra* translated by Charles Luk.

12 Quoted from *What the Bleep Do We Know!?*.

13 This quote of the Buddha comes from one of the 426 verses of the Dhammapada, which is part of a sutra collection on the basics of the Buddha's teachings. See *Dhammapada,* translated by Thomas Byrum.

14 Quoted from page 97 in *The Holotropic Mind* by Stanislav Grof and Hal Tina Bennett.

BIBLIOGRAPHY

Aitken, Robert. *Encouraging Words.* New York: Pantheon, 1993.

Alvarez, Luis. *Alvarez: Adventures of a Physicist.* New York: Basic Books, 1987.

Aristotle. *The Nicomachean Ethics.* London: Penguin Classics, 2004.

Arntz, William, Betsy Chasse, and Mark Vicente. *What the Bleep Do We Know!?* Deerfield Beach, Fla.: Health Communications, 2005.

Bankei. *Bankei Zen.* Translated by Peter Haskel. New York: Grove Weidenfeld, 1984.

Bennett-Goleman, Tara. *Emotional Alchemy: How the Mind Can Heal the Heart.* New York: Three Rivers Press, 2001.

Bly, Robert. *A Little Book on the Human Shadow.* San Francisco: HarperSan Francisco, 1988.

Bohr, Niels. *Atomic Physics and Human Knowledge.* New York: John Wiley and Sons, 1958.

Brach, Tara. *Radical Acceptance: Embracing Your Life with the Heart of a Buddha.* New York: Bantam, 2004.

Buksbazen, John Daishin. *Zen Meditation in Plan English*. Boston: Wisdom Publications, 2002.

Byrum, Thomas. *Dhammapada*. Boston: Shambhala Publications, 1993.

Chodron, Pema. *The Places that Scare You: A Guide to Fearlessness in Difficult Times*. Boston: Shambhala Publications, 2005.

Chopra, Deepak. *Quantum Healing: Exploring the Frontiers of Mind/Body Medicine*. New York: Bantam Books, 1990.

Cleary, Thomas, trans. *Secrets of the Blue Cliff Record*. Boston: Shambhala Publications, 2000.

Conze, E., ed. *On Mahayana Buddhism*. New York: Harper & Row, 1968.

Cook, Frances Dojun. *How to Raise an Ox*. Boston: Wisdom Publications, 2002.

Cousins, Norman. *Anatomy of an Illness as Perceived by the Patient: Reflections on Healing and Regeneration*. New York: Norton, 1979.

Dalai Lama. *The Compassionate Life*. Boston: Wisdom Publications, 2003.

Dogen, Eihei. *Dogen's Extensive Record: A Translation of Eihei Koroju*. Translated by Taigen Dan Leighton and Shohaku Okumura. Boston: Wisdom Publications, 2004.
———. *Moon in a Dewdrop: Writings of Zen Master Dogen*. Edited by Kazuaki Tanahashi. San Francisco: North Point Press, 1995.
———. *Shobogenzo*. Translated by Kosen Nishiyama & John Stevens. 4 vols. Sensai, Japan: Daihokkaikaku, 1975.

Dogen, Eihei and Francis Dojun Cook. *How to Raise an Ox*. Boston: Wisdom Publications, 2002.

Dossey, Larry. *Healing Words: The Power of Prayer and the Practice of Medicine*. San Francisco: HarperSan Francisco, 1993.

Eckhart, Meister. *Meister Eckhart: A Modern Translation*. Translated by William B. Blakney. New York: HarperCollins, 1957.

Einstein, Albert. *Albert Einstein: Philosopher-Scientist*. Edited by P. A. Schlipp. Evanston, Ill.: The Library of Living Philosophers, 1949.
————. *Ideas and Opinions*. New York: Crown Publishers, 1954.

Epstein, Mark. *Thoughts without a Thinker*. New York: Basic Books, 1995.

Gendlin, Eugene. *Focusing*. New York: Bantam Books, 1981.

Glassman, Bernie. *Bearing Witness: A Zen Master's Lesson in Making Peace*. New York: Harmony/Bell Tower, 1999.
————. *Infinite Circle: Teachings in Zen*. Boston: Shambhala Publications, 2002.

Goleman, Daniel. *Emotional Intelligence*. New York: Bantam Books, 1995.

Grof, Stanislav. *Psychology of the Future: Lessons from Modern Consciousness Research*. Albany: State University of New York Press, 2000.

Grof, Stanislav with Hal Zina Bennett. *The Holographic Mind: The Three Levels of Human Consciousness and How They Shape our Lives*. San Francisco: HarperSan Francisco, 1993.

Hakuin Ekaku and Norman Waddell, trans. *Wild Ivy: The Spiritual Autobiography of Zen Master Hakuin*. Boston: Shambhala Publications, 2001.

Hanh, Thich Nhat. *Creating True Peace*. New York: Free Press, 2003.

Hesse, Hermann. *Siddhartha*. New York: Bantam Classics, 1982.
————. *Damien*. New York: Dover Publications, 2000.

Huxley, Aldous. *The Perennial Philosophy: An Interpretation of the Great Mystics, East and West*. New York: Perennial, HarperCollins, 2004.

James, William. *Varieties of Religious Experience*. New York: Modern Library, 1936.

Jung, C. G. *The Archetypes and the Collective Unconscious*. New York: Routledge, 1991.
————. *Axion: Researches into the Phenomenology of the Self*. Princeton, N.J.: Princeton University Press, 1969.

———. *The Collected Works of C. G. Jung.* Vol. 11, *Psychology and Religion: East and West.* Princeton, N.J.: Princeton University Press, 1957.

———. *Memories, Dreams, Reflections.* New York: Vintage Books, 1989.

———. *The Undiscovered Self.* Princeton, N.J.: Princeton University Press, 1990.

Kapleau, Philip. *The Three Pillars of Zen.* Boston: Beacon Press, 1965.

———. *Zen Dawn in the West.* New York: Anchor Books, 1980.

Koestler, Arthur. *Act of Creation.* London: Penguin Books, 1989.

Kornfield, Jack. *A Path with Heart: A Guide Through the Perils and Promises of Spiritual Life.* New York: Bantam Books, 1993.

Kurtz, Ron. *Body-Centered Psychotherapy: The Hakomi Method.* Mendocino, Calif.: Life Rhythm, 1990.

Lowen, Alexander. *Joy: The Surrender to the Body and to Life.* New York: Penguin Compass, 1995.

———. *Bioenergetics.* New York: Penguin Compass, 1994.

Luk, Charles, trans. *The Vimalakirti Nirdesa Sutra.* Berkeley: Shambhala Publications, 1972.

Maezumi, Hakuyu Taizan. *Appreciate Your Life: The Essence of Zen Practice.* Boston: Shambhala Publications, 2001.

———. *The Way of Everyday Life.* Los Angeles: Center Publications, 1978.

Maslow, Abraham. *Religions, Values, and Peak Experiences.* New York: Penguin Books, 1994.

Merzel, Dennis Genpo. *The Eye Never Sleeps.* Boston: Shambhala Publications, 1991.

Milarepa. *The Hundred Thousand Songs of Milarepa.* Boston: Shambhala Publications, 1999.

Nishida, Tenko. *A New Road to Ancient Truth.* New York: Horizon, 1972.

Pagels, Elaine. *Beyond Belief: The Secret Gospel of Thomas.* New York: Random House, 2003.

———. *The Origins of Satan.* New York: Vintage, 1996.

Pert, Candace. *Molecules of Emotion: The Science Behind Mind-Body Medicine*. New York: Scribner, 1999.

Pierrakos, Eva and Donovan, Thesenga. *Fear No Evil*. Del Mar, Calif.: Pathwork Press, 1993.

Pierrakos, John. *Core Energetics: Developing the Capacity to Love and Heal*. Mendocino, Calif.: LifeRhythms, 1990.

Rahula, Walpola. *What the Buddha Taught*. New York: Grove Press, 1974.

Ramakrishna. *The Gospel of Sri Ramakrishna*. New York: Ramakrishna-Vivekananda Center, 1942.

Reps, Paul. *Zen Flesh, Zen Bones: A Collection of Zen and Pre-Zen Writings*. New York: Doubleday, 1989.

Rilke, Rainer Maria. *Letters to a Young Poet*. Translated by M. D. Herter Norton W.W. Norton & Company, 2004.
———. *The Book of Hours: Love Poems to God*. New York: Riverhead Books, 1997.

Rumi. *Teachings of Rumi (The Masnavi): The Spiritual Couplets of Jalaludin Rumi*. Translated by E. M. Whinfield. London: Octagon Press, 1994.
———. *The Essential Rumi*. Translated by Coleman Barks with Hohn Moyne. Edison, N.J.: Castle Books, 1997.
———. *Mathnawi of Jalaluddin Rumi*. Edited by Reynold A. Nicholson. Cambridge, U.K.: Gibb Memorial Trust, 1990.

Saint-Exupéry, Antoine de. *The Little Prince*. San Diego: Harcourt, 2000.

Schlipp, P. A., ed. *Albert Einstein: Philosopher-Scientist*. Evanston, Ill.: The Library of Living Philosophers, 1949.

Schrödinger, Erwin. *Mind and Matter*. Cambrgidge, U.K.: Cambridge University Press, 1958.

Shaku, Soyen. *Sermons of a Buddhist Abbot: The Classic of American Buddhism*. New York: Three Leaves Press/Doubleday, 2004.
———. *Zen for Americans*. New York: Dorset Press, 1987.

Shibayama, Zenkei. *Zen Comments on the Mumonkan*. New York: Harper & Row, 1974.

Shildrick, Margrit. *Embodying the Monster: Encounters with the Vulnerable Self.* London: Sage Publications, 2002.

Shimano, Eido, ed. *Like a Dream, Like a Fantasy.* Boston: Wisdom Publications, 2005.

Tagore, Rabindranath. *Gitanjali*. New York: Scribner, 1997.

Tolle, Eckhart. *A New Earth: Awakening to Your Life's Purpose.* New York: Dutton, 2005.

Vankeerberghen, Griet. *The Huainanzi and Liu An's Claim to Moral Authority.* Albany: State University of New York Press, 2001.

Watson, Burton, trans. *The Lotus Sutra.* New York: Columbia University Press, 1993.

Watts, Alan. *Tao: The Watercourse Way*. New York: Pantheon, 1977.

Welwood, John. *Toward a Psychology of Awakening: Buddhism, Psychotherapy, and the Path of Personal and Spiritual Transformation.* Boston: Shambhala Publications, 2000.

Wick, Gerry Shishin. *The Book of Equanimity: Illuminating Classic Zen Koans.* Boston: Wisdom Publications, 2005.

Wilber, Ken, ed. *Quantum Questions.* Boston: Shambhala Publications, 1984.

Wolf, Fred Alan. *Mind into Matter: A New Alchemy of Science and Spirit.* Portsmouth, N.H.: Moment Point Press, 2000.

INDEX

About Wisdom Publications

Wisdom Publications, a nonprofit publisher, is dedicated to making available authentic works relating to Buddhism for the benefit of all. We publish books by ancient and modern masters in all traditions of Buddhism, translations of important texts, and original scholarship. Additionally, we offer books that explore East-West themes unfolding as traditional Buddhism encounters our modern culture in all its aspects. Our titles are published with the appreciation of Buddhism as a living philosophy, and with the special commitment to preserve and transmit important works from Buddhism's many traditions.

To learn more about Wisdom, or to browse books online, visit our website at www.wisdompubs.org.

You may request a copy of our catalog online or by writing to this address:

Wisdom Publications
199 Elm Street
Somerville, Massachusetts 02144 USA
Telephone: 617-776-7416
Fax: 617-776-7841
Email: info@wisdompubs.org
www.wisdompubs.org

The Wisdom Trust

As a nonprofit publisher, Wisdom is dedicated to the publication of Dharma books for the benefit of all sentient beings and dependent upon the kindness and generosity of sponsors in order to do so. If you would like to make a donation to Wisdom, you may do so through our website or our Somerville office. If you would like to help sponsor the publication of a book, please write or email us at the address above.

Thank you.

Wisdom is a nonprofit, charitable 501(c)(3) organization affiliated with the Foundation for the Preservation of the Mahayana Tradition (FPMT).